TABLE OF CONTENTS

Unless otherwise indicated, all Scripture quotations are taken from the King James Version of the Bible.

The Assignment: The Trials & The Triumphs, Volume 3
ISBN 1-56394-055-8
Copyright © 1999 by *MIKE MURDOCK*
All publishing rights belong exclusively to Wisdom International
Published by The Wisdom Center · P.O. Box 99 · Denton, Texas 76202
1-888-WISDOM-1 (1-888-947-3661) · Website: www.thewisdomcenter.cc

Stop Looking At
Where You Have Been
And Start Looking At
Where You Can Be.

-MIKE MURDOCK

❧ 1 ❧

EVERY ASSIGNMENT HAS BIRTHPLACE.

Every Assignment Begins Somewhere.

Over the years, I have listened to extraordinary men of God speak. They can trace turning points of their life to a specific hour, a date, and a particular geographical place they were standing or kneeling.

This has happened in my own life. I can take you to the very spot where I first felt the call to preach the gospel. I was just four years old. It was in my father's church in Orange, Texas. A precious and godly woman, Lillian Logan, prayed for me. That morning in children's church, it was like fire inside me. I wept as I laid my little hands on the backs of the other children and prayed for them.

It happened again in Waco, Texas. I was just eight years old. I remember the moment. Even though the church has since been torn down, I remember where I was kneeling. Tears streamed down my face. I promised God, "I will go where you want me to go and be anything you want me to be."

Another life changing event occurred when I was fifteen years old. A great pastor, Fred Hill, was preaching at a camp meeting in Lake Arthur, Louisiana. In one of his sermons, he told a story about a little boy who came by the church every morning to pray for his parents who were not Christians. One morning after prayer, the pastor heard a crash and ran out to discover an automobile wreck outside the church door. The little boy had been killed.

At the funeral, both parents were saved. The pastor made this statement, *"The little boy did not live a long life, but he did live a full one."*

It tore me apart inside. I wept and sobbed the entire day. I had always felt like my time on earth was limited, and that I would not live out a full 70- or 100-year life span. That day I made a total commitment to God that however long my life might be, it would definitely be a *full* life—it would be dedicated to His glory.

Another turning point occurred when I was 18 years old in Bible school. A great missionary, R. L. Brandt, preached on the subject, "Burn your plow." He related that Elisha was *following* Elijah. Elisha had to stop his farming, *burn his plow* (his dependency upon his oxen for his financial income), and focus on his mentor's mantle.

As I listened that morning in chapel, conviction gripped me. You see, I had often felt that my financial income would derive from *business*. I would preach on *weekends*.

That day I surrendered to full-time ministry.

I spent the entire day weeping, laying on my face in that chapel. I felt that my heart was being torn out of my chest. I knew that total surrender meant that I could no longer depend on a business for my financial support. I had to be willing to empty myself completely to reach others with the gospel. Then, my trust in God would be validated and *rewarded*.

That was one of the most difficult days in my entire life. That was a time of very traumatic change in my life—I will always remember exactly *where* it took place.

The greatest day of my life was July 13, 1994.

I went to bed at 5:00 a.m. on Wednesday morning, July 13, 1994. I thought I would sleep in until 10:00 or 11:00 in the morning. But, after only two hours, at 7:00 a.m., I was awakened by the Holy Spirit.

I fell in love with Him that day.

The Holy Spirit forever changed my life and ministry. The Holy Spirit was so powerful and strong in my room that I was compelled to go to prayer. That day birthed an obsession—to intimately *know* the Person of the Holy Spirit—not just His power.

Since that day, I have held Schools of the Holy Spirit throughout the nation. I have found the Holy Spirit to be the only true Source of constant joy, and the only true Source of unchanging peace.

When I please Him, joy dominates me.

When I offend Him, He withdraws.

God will schedule uncommon experiences for you—you can have your own Bethel, Upper Room experiences, and specific *places* that signal a total change in the direction of your life.

Document them.

Always celebrate turning points.

It is important for you to attach significance to the places where God speaks to you.

As I write these words to you, it is midnight on Wednesday. Here in the privacy of my little Wisdom Room in my home, the Holy Spirit has just nudged my heart to pray a special prayer for you, that your reading of this Volume on "The Assignment" will become the turning point of your life.

It is not a coincidence that this book is in your hand this very moment.

Your Assignment has a birthplace. Reading this book will be the beginning of a clear and understandable photograph of your Assignment on earth.

Our Prayer Together...

"Precious Holy Spirit, though it is late tonight as I am writing these words to my precious friend, You have stirred my heart to pray a special prayer. I ask You, in the holy name of Jesus of Nazareth, to touch my friend dramatically while he reads these words. Reveal clearly once and forever *the path to his Assignment.* Unmuddy his waters. Unclutter his life. Strip away from him every option and alternative to Your perfect plan. *Remove the distraction* from his life that breaks his focus. I decree from the north, the south, the east, and the west, wonderful and rewarding people will step out of the shadows of his life and raise his arms during his personal battle for significance. Just as Aaron and Hur held up the hands of Moses during battle, place supportive relationships around him in the name of Jesus. Do this now. Holy Spirit, I ask You to walk beside my friend today. Carefully and methodically move him toward the *center* of his life Assignment. Unleash a new flow of energy and enthusiasm within them, so that he will embrace his Assignment with great joy and with new vigor and vitality. It is done this very hour. This is the birth place for his Assignment once and forever, in Jesus' name. Amen."

Remember: *Every Assignment Has A Birthplace.*

❧ 2 ❧

YOUR ASSIGNMENT WILL ALWAYS ENABLE SOMEONE ELSE TO SUCCEED.

Somebody Is Waiting For You.

These Scriptures have greatly affected my life:

▶ "Knowing that whatsoever good thing any man doeth, the same shall he receive of the Lord, whether he be bond or free" (Eph. 6:8).

▶ "Withhold not good from them to whom it is due, when it is in the power of thine hand to do it" (Prov. 3:27).

▶ "The Spirit of the Lord God is upon me; because the Lord hath anointed me to preach good tidings unto the meek; He hath sent me to bind up the broken-hearted, to proclaim liberty to the captives, and the opening of the prison to them that are bound" (Isa. 61:1-3).

Someone Should Succeed Because Of You.

Note that His empowering is to help other people around you *enter their Season of Greatness*.

The Assignment of *Ruth* was to Naomi. She was involved in Naomi's survival.

The Assignment of *David* was to help Saul and

the Israelites enter victory. When he killed Goliath, he helped keep the nation of Israel free from domination by its enemies.

The Assignment of *Joseph* was the survival of the nation and his family. When Joseph interpreted Pharaoh's dream accurately, it enabled him to help his own family and thousands of people to survive through seven years of famine.

When *Job* prayed for his friends, God turned his own captivity and restored him.

Your Assignment has little to do with your personal survival. It has much to do with helping others achieve total obedience to God's instructions. *When you help them, God gets involved with your life.*

As I was speaking on a telethon recently, the Holy Spirit spoke to me to tell the people something very powerful: "When you get involved with God's dream, He will get involved with *your* dream. When you get involved with what is on God's mind, He will get involved with what is on *your* mind. When the widow of Zarephath concentrated on the needs of the prophet—God concentrated on *her* needs."

It is quite true, *"What You Make Happen For Others, God Will Make Happen For You"* (Eph. 6:8).

When I talk to people about their Assignment, I always ask them this question: "Who is surviving today because of what you did last year?"

Remember: *Your Assignment Will Always Enable Someone Else To Succeed.*

3

YOUR ASSIGNMENT MAY BE REVEALED BY GOD THROUGH A DREAM.

God Often Speaks Through Dreams.

There are many strange occurrences in our lives that are unexplainable. Some dreams occur because you ate too much pizza at 2:00 a.m.! Other dreams occur because of a mixture of imaginations and fantasies we have entertained. However, some dreams come directly from God.

God has spoken to me through dreams on numerous occasions.

6 Important Facts You Should Remember About Dreams

1. *God Gave Joseph Dreams Of His Leadership And Promotion Years Before He Became Second In Command Of Egypt.* "And Joseph dreamed a dream, and he told it his brethren" (Gen. 37:5).

2. *The Life Of Jesus Was Preserved By The Impartation Of A Dream.*

Joseph, the earthly father of Jesus, received divine instructions through a dream. "And when they were departed, behold, the angel of the Lord appeareth to Joseph in a dream, saying, Arise, and take the young child and his mother, and flee into Egypt, and be thou there until I bring thee word: for Herod will seek the young child to destroy Him" (Matt. 2:13).

3. *Solomon Experienced Radical Changes Through The Flow Of Wisdom That Began Through A Dream.* "In Gibeon the Lord appeared to Solomon in a dream by night: and God said, Ask what I shall give thee." And Solomon answered Him, saying, "Give therefore Thy servant an understanding heart to judge Thy people...And God said unto him...lo, I have given thee a wise and an understanding heart; so that there was none like thee before thee, neither after thee shall any arise like unto thee" (see 1 Kings 3:5,9-14).

4. *It Is Wise To Document Your Dreams.* Especially give attention to those which reoccur. Do not build your entire lifestyle around a dream, but rather let the dream be a motivation to pursue the presence of God and secure a clear-cut interpretation of what He revealed through that dream.

5. *Time Will Reveal The Validity Of Any God-Given Dream.* Several years ago, a young lady listened raptly as I spoke at a church here in Dallas. Afterwards, she came up to me and said, "I am assigned to you. Someday I am going to work for you and be your secretary."

"That is nice. I am certain God will guide your steps," I replied quietly.

To my surprise I arrived home a few weeks later and found she had become the secretary for my office manager. One day she whispered excitedly to me, "I still know I am assigned to you. I will be your personal secretary someday."

A few weeks later, through an unexpected turn of events, that position opened, and she was the one most qualified to fill it. She was excited. I thought, "Well, this is something! She said months ago that she was assigned to me. We shall see."

After thirty days of intense work and effort, she suddenly resigned. She could not handle the stress and strong demands of the position. I did not see her again for several years. Was she really assigned to me? Of course not.

6. *Evaluate Prayerfully And Patiently Any Dream You Believe To Be Divinely Inspired.* God gives us dreams to prepare us for a new season to increase our flexibility for making changes and move us closer to the center of our Assignment.

Remember: *Your Assignment May Be Revealed By God Through A Dream.*

You Will Only Have
Significant Success
With Something
That Is An Obsession.

-MIKE MURDOCK

⪘ 4 ⪘

YOUR OBSESSION WITH YOUR ASSIGNMENT DETERMINES THE SUCCESS OF YOUR ASSIGNMENT.

Success Requires Your Decision.
Failure merely requires your permission.

3 Necessary Elements In The Completion Of Your Assignment

▶ *Awareness* of your Assignment.
▶ *Development* of your Assignment.
▶ *Obsession* with your Assignment.

Your awareness of your Assignment may come through your parents. Samuel was a remarkable young man raised in the temple under the priest, Eli. He was one of the greatest men in the Old Testament. He anointed Saul. He anointed David to follow the kingship of Saul.

Hannah, the mother of Samuel, was one of the most remarkable women of the Old Testament. She wept and sobbed in the temple. "And she was in bitterness of soul, and prayed unto the Lord, and wept sore" (1 Sam. 1:10). This woman craved a child.

She craved a man child, a *son.*

She was willing to take a vow to make it happen. It was a vow of isolation, loss, and separation from the son. "And she vowed a vow, and said, O Lord of hosts, if Thou wilt indeed look on the affliction of Thine handmaid, and remember me, and not forget Thine handmaid, but wilt give unto Thine handmaid a man child, then I will give him unto the Lord all the days of his life, and there shall no razor come upon his head" (1 Sam. 1:11).

Wise parents continuously mentor their children regarding their Assignment. Hannah brought Samuel to Eli. "And when she had weaned him, she took him up with her, with three bullocks, and one ephah of flour, and a bottle of wine, and brought him unto the house of the Lord in Shiloh: and the child was young. And they slew a bullock, and brought the child to Eli. And she said, Oh my lord, as thy soul liveth, my lord, I am the woman that stood by thee here, praying unto the Lord. For this child I prayed; and the Lord hath given me my petition which I asked of Him: Therefore also I have lent him to the Lord; as long as he liveth he shall be lent to the Lord. And he worshipped the Lord there" (1 Sam. 1:24-28).

> ▶ She explained her isolation from her son.
> ▶ She made Samuel aware of her vow and that he belonged now to God.

He was *required* to develop a life focused on the presence of God.

6 Action Steps In Developing An Obsession For Your Assignment

1. *Develop And Prepare For Your*

Assignment. You are not *born* qualified—you must *become* qualified. Jesus took 30 years. Moses took 80 years. Preparation requires mentors, diligence, and focus. "And Jesus increased in Wisdom and stature, and in favour with God and man" (Luke 2:52).

2. *Develop An Obsession For Your Assignment.* The Apostle Paul is a perfect example. "Brethren, I count not myself to have apprehended: but this one thing I do, forgetting those things which are behind, and reaching forth unto those things which are before, I press toward the mark for the prize of the high calling of God in Christ Jesus" (Phil. 3:13,14).

3. *Become Ruthless In Removing Any Distractions To Your Assignment.* "So likewise, whosoever he be of you that forsaketh not all that he hath, he cannot be My disciple" (Luke 14:33). "For where your treasure is, there will your heart be also" (Luke 12:34).

4. *Never Consider Any Option To Your Assignment.* "And Jesus said unto him, No man, having put his hand to the plough, and looking back, is fit for the kingdom of God" (Luke 9:62).

5. *Expect God To Send Someone To You Who Makes You Aware Of Your Assignment.* Abigail stirred the mind of David by reminding him of his destined place on the throne. He changed his plan from killing Nabal and his servants to awaiting God's timing (read 1 Sam. 25).

6. *Anticipate God Moving Quickly To Complete His Assignment Through You.* "Then said the Lord unto me, Thou hast well seen: for I will hasten My Word to perform it" (Jer. 1:12).

One of the greatest healing evangelists in the

world has often said, "God spoke to me and instructed me to bring his healing power to my generation." His *awareness* of his Assignment and his *obsession* to pray for the sick has created incredible success in his ministry.

If you succeed, it will happen because of your personal decision to obey God's voice.

If you fail, it will be through deliberate disobedience or ignorance of His plan for your life.

Nobody else is responsible for you. You are responsible for your own Assignment. Move quickly toward it.

Your *daily appointments* should reveal your obsession with your Assignment.

Your *friendships* should reflect your obsession with your Assignment.

Your *conversations* should revolve around your Assignment.

Remember: *Your Obsession With Your Assignment Determines The Success Of Your Assignment.*

≈ 5 ≈

YOUR ASSIGNMENT MAY REQUIRE UNCOMMON KNOWLEDGE IN A SPECIFIC FIELD OF STUDY.

You Are Not Born Qualified.

You *become* qualified for your Assignment.

If God has called you to go overseas, study the culture, customs, and language of that particular country.

If God has assigned you to the academic world, there may be areas of unique study that you have not even dreamed about pursuing. You must prepare yourself.

Qualification requires dedication. Prepare to focus hours of study and hard work. Be prepared to give up everything to complete God's Assignment in your life.

Do you really want to succeed in your Assignment? What are the necessary areas of study you must pursue?

It is quite interesting. Everywhere I go, people approach me and say, "I am called into the ministry. I cannot wait until God frees me from my secular job to go pursue His calling."

"Wonderful! I have an annual three-day School of Ministry at the Wisdom Center, and I would love to help train you for the ministry. It contains many hours of practical application in what you can presently do to move into your next season. Are you interested in coming?" I ask.

"Uh, uh, I will think about it. Right now, I am very involved in my business and building an extra room on my house. I am not sure I have enough money to fly to Dallas."

They are not taking their Assignment seriously. Or, they are totally mistaken about it.

I would not want anyone to work on my car who is unqualified.

I do not want anyone repairing my computers who is unqualified.

I do not want anyone teaching me the Word of God who is unqualified.

If you are unwilling to pursue knowledge of your Assignment, do not expect to succeed.

Remember: *Your Assignment May Require Uncommon Knowledge In A Specific Field Of Study.*

≈ 6 ≈

BECAUSE NOBODY ELSE HAS RECEIVED YOUR ASSIGNMENT, NOBODY ELSE UNDERSTANDS IT LIKE YOU DO.

Nobody Like You Has Ever Existed Before.

Nobody knows your Assignment like you do. This is why it is so important to find the center of your anointing and stay there. *Learn* your Assignment. *Focus* on it. Narrow down your life to build around it. Unclutter your life and get rid of anything that does not contribute to your Assignment. Do not dabble in everything. Specialize in what God has told you to do with your life. *Do it better than anyone else.* Do what you do best.

When I was fifteen years old, an extraordinary preacher came to visit our church. He was a magnificent and articulate speaker. I asked him to share with me important thoughts about the ministry. I will never forget it.

"First, anyone who reads less than 20 chapters a day of the Bible is not qualified to call himself a man of God," he said quite boldly.

So, at age 15, I began carefully studying 20 chapters of the Bible every day. I emptied myself into the Word of God, outlining five sermons per day from what I had read.

"How do you get such confidence when you get up to preach?" I asked.

"If I am going to speak on prayer," he answered, "I soak myself in prayer. I study the concordance and read every single Scripture I can find on the subject. I memorize Scriptures on prayer. I eat, drink, and talk prayer 24 hours a day. I read every book written by great men of prayer. I find out their habits, their lifestyle, and their comments. By the time I walk into the pulpit, I know more about prayer than any person sitting in front of me.

"Now, the audience does not even know what I am going to speak on that night. They have been on their jobs working as electricians, or engineers, or taxicab drivers. I have been studying *prayer.* I am many hours and many weeks *ahead of them.*

"I know that if any of them knew more about prayer than I do, God would have them in the pulpit instead of me. *So, when I get up to speak I am very aware that I know more about my subject than anyone else present.* That gives me boldness and confidence in my speaking."

This also explains why some of us do not succeed in our life. We are working on jobs that are not the *center* of our expertise. Perhaps we simply love our boss. Perhaps we just need work. We require finances to pay the bills, so we accept the first job available near our home.

This is tragic. Your Assignment should be

unique to you. You cannot please anybody but the Lord. People will pull on you, trying to get you to follow their instructions. They will make demands on your time, your money, and your attention. The only way to hear God's voice about your Assignment is to spend time alone with Him. Then empty yourself into what He told you to do with your life.

When God Places A Mantle On You, Nobody Else Can Do What You Do.

Remember: *Because Nobody Else Has Received Your Assignment, Nobody Else Understands It Like You Do.*

Give Another
What He Cannot Find
Anywhere Else And
He Will Keep Returning.

-MIKE MURDOCK

❧ 7 ❧

YOUR ASSIGNMENT WILL BECOME YOUR LEGACY TO OTHERS.

You Will Be Remembered For Something.

When you hear the name Allan Greenspan, you think of the economy.

When you hear the name Adolph Hitler, you think of the holocaust.

▶ Your Assignment must become your *obsession*.

▶ Your Obsession will become your *legacy*.

▶ Your Legacy is the way you will be *remembered*.

Think for one moment. When you remember your mother, what one word describes her? When you think about your father, what one word describes him? When your children think about you, what one word will describe you?

Your life is not over.

You can make changes *today*.

Yes, even while you are reading this book, you can make significant changes in your life.

You can decide your legacy.

How do you want to be remembered by those closest to you? What is your plan for your future?

What will be your legacy to those who follow after you? What provisions have you made for your influence to continue after you are gone? When people discuss you, what are the most common words they use? Who do you want to carry your mantle? Are you doing something worth perpetuating? Who are you training to take your place, carry your torch, and create changes in the next generation?

You Will Be Remembered In Life For Two Things: The Problems You Solve Or The Ones You Create.

Jonas Salk will be remembered for the vaccine he discovered to cure polio. Mother Theresa is remembered for pouring her life out to the poor. Billy Graham will be remembered for the simplicity of the salvation messages he gave to millions. These great individuals solved problems.

This is their legacy—the way they are remembered.

12 Good Things About Problems

▶ *Your Assignment is to solve a problem.*
▶ The problem you solve is your legacy to others.
▶ Problems around you are the Golden Keys to favor.
▶ Problems can be marvelous, mysterious, and wonderful Beginnings.
▶ Problems are the golden hinges on the Door of Relationship.
▶ Problems are Gateways to significance.
▶ Problems make people *reach* for each other.
▶ Problems create *humility*, forcing you to

see the value of those around you.
▶ Problems begin new seasons.
▶ Your problem has birthed your financial income.
▶ *When you solve a problem, you create a reward.*
▶ *When you solve a problem for others, God guarantees your own prosperity* (Isa. 58:10,11).

You are commanded and expected to solve problems for others. "Withhold not good from them to whom it is due, when it is in the power of thine hand to do it" (Prov. 3:27).

Focus only on the problems you are assigned to solve. Eliminate trivia from your day. Do not try to do too many things. Concentrate on pouring your life into a narrow focus, to solve the most significant problem possible for those closest to you.

Today can be the beginning of your greatness.

Remember: *Your Assignment Will Become Your Legacy To Others.*

Your Seed Is Anything
That Benefits Another.
Your Harvest Is Anything
That Benefits You.

-MIKE MURDOCK

8

You Will Only Be Remembered For Your Obsession.

The Persuaded Are Persuasive.

This is a strong statement. It is worthy of you sitting down this very moment while reading this book and contemplating, "What do I want to be *remembered* for?"

When you remember Alexander Graham Bell, you think about the telephone.

When you remember Thomas Edison, you think about the electric light bulb.

When you remember Henry Ford, you think about the automobile.

When you remember the Wright brothers, you think about the airplane.

When you remember Kathryn Kuhlman, you think about miracles.

When you remember George Washington, you think about the father of our country.

You will only succeed with something that has become an obsession.

Everything extraordinary began as a passion, a vision, an obsession.

Note anything that has the ability to keep your

attention.

> ► Anything That Can Keep Your Attention Is Capable Of Mastering You.
> ► Focus Creates Mastery.
> ► What You Look At The Longest Will Become The Strongest In Your Life.

Some attempt careers in real estate. Yet, they hate to go to real estate seminars. They refuse to be mentored by someone who is already successful in that field. They refuse to invest inconvenient hours in showing properties to potential clients. Yet, they wonder why they do not succeed.

Late one night, I listened as two pastors of small churches discussed the reasons why their congregations remained small. It was interesting. One felt that it was because he "preached too straight."

When they finished talking I said quite simply, "Neither one of you has ever attended any church growth conferences. You buy houses and real estate and cars, yet you have never purchased an airline ticket to go and sit at the feet of a church authority who took a congregation to 4,000 people. Having 1,000 church members is not important to you because it has not become your obsession."

Your passion will become your legacy.

Remember: *You Will Only Be Remembered For Your Obsession.*

≈ 9 ≈

YOU WILL NEVER SEE THE MIRACLE HAND OF GOD IN ANYTHING YOU ATTEMPT WITHOUT HIM.

Your Assignment Will Require Miracles.

When God gives you an Assignment, it will require Him.

Never attempt anything great without God.

If God has not led you concerning your new business, do not start it.

If God has not led you into your relationship, stay single. Years ago, I was greatly pressured by friends to become engaged. Though I was not really "in love," I cared deeply for her. But, it was not right. In fact, I was not at all at peace that she was the person to marry. I permitted everyone else around me to talk me into the engagement.

The next morning my heart felt like ten thousand pounds of lead had been emptied on it. I had never known such a sudden lack of joy. I knew I had made a mistake. I had not received God's approval, but merely men's approval.

The approval of God is very necessary for anything you want to work in your life. Do not *force* relationships. *Let* them grow.

Provision is only guaranteed for the Assignment God has commanded.

Church leaders, please read this carefully. Satan is choking the life of the church through debt. One of the saddest pictures emerging is men of God who plunge their churches into debt, spending money that has never yet arrived. It seems a total contradiction to the instructions of the Word, "thou shalt not borrow" (Deut. 28:12).

Whatever you are considering, if God is not in it, *refuse to do it.* Without the presence and blessing of the Lord, it will not bring you joy, but heartache.

Every command contains a plan. Find it.

Remember: *You Will Never See The Miracle Hand Of God In Anything You Attempt Without Him.*

≈ 10 ≈

EVERY STEP TOWARD SELF-SUFFICIENCY IS A STEP AWAY FROM GOD.

God Will Not Permit You To Succeed Without Him.

Many years ago I began to write songs. It was astounding how God blessed me. Suddenly people everywhere were recording my songs. I received tens of thousands of dollars in royalties.

Because I owned my own publishing company, I received double royalty as a composer and publisher. It was not long before I had built up quite a nest egg. I decided I would live off the interest the savings would generate.

One day in prayer, God spoke to me and said, *"Every step toward self-sufficiency is a step away from Me."* To this very day, I have never forgotten that word of warning.

God rewards faith, not brilliance. Moses wrote, "When thou hast eaten and art full, then thou shalt bless the Lord thy God for the good land which he hath given thee" (Deut. 8:10). Then Moses went on to say, "And thou say in thine heart, My power and the might of mine hand hath gotten me this wealth. *But thou shalt remember the Lord thy God:* for it is

He that giveth thee power to get wealth, that He may establish His covenant which He sware unto thy fathers, as it is this day." (Deut. 8:17,18)

Our efforts are often attempts to create a lifestyle that will make God unnecessary. He will not permit that.

His Only Pleasure Is To Be Believed.

His Only Pain Is To Be Doubted.

Without faith, it truly is impossible to please the Lord.

You cannot succeed alone. "Not that we are sufficient of ourselves to think any thing as of ourselves; but our sufficiency is of God" (2 Cor. 3:5). "Not of works, lest any man should boast" (Eph. 2:9).

God has tested me numerous times. One Monday evening in a crusade, the Lord spoke to me and told me to give the entire offering to the pastor of the church where I was preaching. I did.

Tuesday night, God instructed me to ask for eight people to plant a Seed of $1,000 in our ministry. After I made the announcement, eight people rushed to the front and stood there waiting. I anointed each of them with oil. We prayed, dedicating that Seed to the Lord. As we were praying, the Lord spoke to me and said, "This is an Isaac offering."

The disappointment that hit my heart was indescribable. You see, an Isaac offering is one when the Lord tells you to do something just to test your obedience. Then I instructed the people, "I know you are here to sow your Seed of $1,000. However, God has just spoken to me that this is an Isaac offering. He just wanted to test your obedience to His voice.

You are to keep your offering, and you will receive one hundredfold in return as if you had actually given it" (read Mark 10:28-30).

It happened again in one of my World Wisdom Conferences here in Dallas. An incredible wave of anointing swept into the service. I felt the Lord instructing me to have people come forward who would plant a Seed of $10,000 in our ministry to spread the gospel. Forty people rushed to the front to plant a $10,000 Seed. As I walked down the row and anointed each one, the Holy Spirit spoke to me and said very clearly, "I want this to be your Isaac offering."

Now, as I just explained, an 'Isaac' offering is when the Lord asks you to do something to test your *willingness.* Do you remember the story of Abraham and Isaac? After God had given Abraham his son Isaac through Sarah, He then asked Abraham to do a very hard thing: to sacrifice Isaac on the mountain.

Just as Abraham was about to kill Isaac, the voice of the Lord came forth. A ram was provided to replace Isaac. God just wanted to test his obedience to see whom he loved the most.

When I told the 40 partners of our ministry that it was an Isaac offering, to keep the $10,000, and that God wanted just to test us, I went back with mixed emotions to my hotel room that night.

"That was $400,000 to buy television air time to spread Your name!" I argued. God spoke deeply into my spirit that night, saying, *"What You Are Willing To Walk Away From Determines What I Will Bring To You."*

Then, He spoke one of the most important

Wisdom Keys that I have ever learned: *"Whatever You Can Walk Away From Is Something You Have Mastered."* Few people grasp this. But it has radically affected my life.

It is good to provide for your own household.

It is wise to plan ahead for your retirement.

It is honorable to carefully manage your money so that God is pleased. But do not ever forget: *Any attempt to isolate your life from acts of faith will be disastrous and will create catastrophes in your life.* Oral Roberts has said it well, "The most dangerous day in your life is the day you don't require a miracle."

God is only impressed by an act of faith.

Remember: *Every Step Toward Self-Sufficiency Is A Step Away From God.*

⁓ 11 ⁓

GOD WILL NEVER ADVANCE YOU BEYOND YOUR LAST ACT OF DISOBEDIENCE.

Disobedience Will Paralyze Your Progress.

The great Israelite leader Joshua experienced this. "So the Lord was with Joshua; and his fame was noised throughout all the country" (Joshua 6:27). Everybody had heard about Joshua. Victories were being collected. The anointing and presence of God was manifest all over Israel.

Suddenly tragedy struck. "But the children of Israel committed a trespass in the accursed thing... and the anger of the Lord was kindled against the children of Israel" (Joshua 7:1).

Disobedience Turns God Into An Enemy.

Joshua had found the winning combination. His leaders were fierce fighters. His fame had been noised abroad. His mantle was secure. His leadership was extraordinary.

Suddenly, everything came apart.

The Israelites lost the battle of Ai. They were crushed. Their reputation unraveled. Joshua raced back to his tent and began to tear his clothes and cry out to the Lord. God then told him the reason they lost the battle. Disobedience was in the camp. One of his men, Achan, had kept some of the spoils from the city of Jericho, in direct disobedience to the Lord's commands.

God Can Become Your Enemy.

God can remove His Hedge of Protection.

Your tears will rush like Niagara Falls.

Your laughter stops.

Your victories become memories.

God can remind you of your frailty *in a single moment.*

This is seldom taught. We have such a "God loves you" philosophy these days, that we have totally forgotten that the severity of the Lord is just as certain as His goodness. Hell is just as certain as heaven.

When The Seeds Of Disobedience Are Planted, The Reward System Begins To Shut Down. Certainly, the mercies of God permit the blessings to fall like occasional rain drops. He attempts to keep you reminded of His mercy and His blessings. But continued disobedience eventually destroys your relationship with God.

That's why mercy often becomes dangerous.

When judgment is delayed, it is often misinterpreted. It is easy to assume that God did not really notice, that obedience is not that important, after all. Then, the judgment comes—swiftly and thoroughly.

My mother taught me an important truth.

"Son, the will of God is really an *attitude*." She continued, "If you get out of the will of God, if you will fall upon your face and cry loud to Him and ask Him to put you back in the center of His plan, in a single moment those blessings can begin to flow again."

Have you failed the Lord? Did you listen to the wrong person and sow a Seed of defiance and rebellion to God's plan? Please embrace this wonderful truth: A broken and contrite spirit He will not despise.

Our Prayer Together...

"Heavenly Father, I recognize my disobedience. I ask You to forgive me this very moment for failing to honor Your voice. I know I have sinned. This is not the direction I want my life to go. I give all of my life, my heart, and my future to You today. Heal me on the inside. Heal my mind, my memories, my life. I embrace You as my Savior, my Lord, and my God. From this moment forward, let Your mercy and peace flow toward me. Let today be the beginning of miraculous changes. From this day forward, I will walk uprightly toward You. In Jesus' name. Amen."

Stay obedient. Too much is at stake.

Remember: *God Will Never Advance You Beyond Your Last Act Of Disobedience.*

Anything That
Does Not Change You
Is Unnecessary
In Your Life.

-MIKE MURDOCK

❧ 12 ❧

YOUR SUCCESS IN YOUR ASSIGNMENT DEPENDS ON YOUR ABILITY TO EMBRACE CORRECTION.

━━━━➤●◄━━━━

Only The Humble Are Correctable.

You do not know everything. Ignorance is devastating. "My people are destroyed for lack of knowledge" (Hosea 4:6).

Your discoveries determine your seasons. The true difference between your present season and your future is information.

Correction hurts—when you try so very hard to do things correctly only to discover that you have made a bad decision. It especially hurts if those who are correcting you appear insensitive or unaware of your efforts.

16 Facts You Should Know About Correction

1. *Correction Was A Major Part Of The Ministry Of Jesus.*

> ▶ *Jesus corrected Peter.* "But He turned, and said unto Peter, Get thee behind Me, satan:

thou art an offence unto Me: for thou savourest not the things that be of God, but those that be of men" (Matt. 16:23).

▶ *Jesus corrected the disciples.* "Afterward He appeared unto the eleven as they sat at meat, and upbraided them with their unbelief and hardness of heart, because they believed not them which had seen Him after He was risen" (Mark 16:14).

▶ *Jesus corrected Pharisees and Scribes.* "Woe unto you, scribes and Pharisees, hypocrites! for ye pay tithe of mint and anise and cummin, and have omitted the weightier matters of the law, judgment, mercy, and faith: these ought ye to have done, and not to leave the other undone" (Matt. 23:23-27).

2. *Those Who Accepted The Correction Of Jesus Are Promised Everlasting Life.* "That if thou shalt confess with thy mouth the Lord Jesus, and shalt believe in thine heart that God hath raised Him from the dead, thou shalt be saved. For with the heart man believeth unto righteousness; and with the mouth confession is made unto salvation" (Rom. 10:9,10).

3. *Those Who Rebelled Against The Correction Of Jesus Are Now Burning In Hell Forever.* "And in hell he lift up his eyes, being in torments, and seeth Abraham afar off, and Lazarus in his bosom." (Luke 16:23).

4. *The Apostle Paul Continuously Corrected Those Under His Spiritual Care.* The love of God within him motivated these letters of encouragement, correction, and order. "All scripture

is given by inspiration of God, and is profitable for doctrine, for reproof, for correction, for instruction in righteousness" (2 Tim. 3:16).

5.   *Prisons Are Filled With People Who Were Unwilling To Respect Correction.* Thousands will never see another rainbow during their lifetime, observe the gorgeous sunrise in the mornings, nor hear the laughter of children for the remainder of their life. Rebellion is always costly. "In the lips of him that hath understanding Wisdom is found: but a rod is for the back of him that is void of understanding" (Prov. 10:13).

6.   *Corrections Should Begin Early In Life.* If you were fortunate enough to have parents who corrected you appropriately and continuously, your chances to succeed have been multiplied. "Train up a child in the way he should go: and when he is old, he will not depart from it" (Prov. 22:6).

7.   *Many Have Lost Valuable Years Of Mentorship Because They Are Unwilling To Take Correction From Their Pastor.* They move from church to church, looking for a "fresh" and new experience through a different man or woman of God. Stability has rewards beyond explanation. "Believe in the Lord your God, so shall ye be established; believe His prophets, so shall ye prosper" (2 Chr. 20:20).

8.   *Correction Is Your Bridge To Promotion.* "Give instruction to a wise man, and he will be yet wiser: teach a just man, and he will increase in learning" (Prov. 9:9).

9.   *Reproof Can Position You Among The Successful.* "The ear that heareth the reproof of life

abideth among the wise" (Prov. 15:31).

10. *When You Refuse Correction, You Destroy Your Own Future And Life.* "He that refuseth instruction despiseth his own soul: but he that heareth reproof getteth understanding" (Prov. 15:32).

11. *Counselors Increase The Potential Of Your Success.* "For by wise counsel thou shalt make thy war: and in multitude of counsellors there is safety" (Prov. 24:6).

12. *Correction Can Eliminate Disappointments In Your Future.* "Without counsel purposes are disappointed: but in the multitude of counsellors they are established" (Prov. 15:22).

13. *Godly Correction Increases Your Successes More Than The Love Of Another.* "Open rebuke is better than secret love" (Prov. 27:5).

14. *You Can Predict The Success Of Your Children By Their Response To Your Correction.* "Correct thy son, and he shall give thee rest; yea, he shall give delight unto thy soul" (Prov. 29:17).

15. *Correction Produces Wisdom In Your Child.* "The rod and reproof give Wisdom: but a child left to himself bringeth his mother to shame" (Prov. 29:15). "He that spareth his rod hateth his son: but he that loveth him chasteneth him betimes" (Prov. 13:24).

16. *Correction Was Encouraged By The Ancient Wise Men.* "Hear instruction, and be wise, and refuse it not" (Prov. 8:33).

It is sometimes difficult to differentiate between correction and criticism. It is often easy to accept correction from a proven mentor or a loyal friend. It is almost impossible to accept correction from a critic, an enemy or someone contemptuous of your Assignment. Accepting correction is the difference between maturity and immaturity.

Many years ago, a great military leader said, "Observe thyself as your enemies would observe you, thus you will become your very best friend." What did he mean? Look carefully at your life in the same way that the most critical, cynical, and sarcastic enemy would examine you in an effort to destroy you. This enables you to discern the weaknesses in your life, your areas of vulnerability where your enemy could potentially destroy you.

Your best ideas may come from your worst enemy. Never forget this. As one of my dear friends, Sherman Owens, often says, "Listen to happy voices for *encouragement.* Listen to unhappy voices for *ideas.*" The unhappy customers are the ones who unlock the wisest changes made by great companies.

Your friends *accept* your weakness.

Your enemies *expose* your weakness.

Your mentor helps *remove* your weakness.

The Correction Checklist

Here is a short checklist to help you extract the most from those difficult, painful, and sometimes tearful sessions of correction:

1. *Is It The Truth?* Truth sets you free. Truth makes change possible. Truth launches seasons of blessing. Correction is merely the painful hinge on the door to extraordinary pleasure. Correction is a moment; promotion can be a lifetime.

2. *If It Is Truthful, How Quickly Can I Make The Needed Change?* Who can encourage and

strengthen me in making the change?

3. *If I Refuse To Accept This Correction, What Is The Worst Scenario That Could Eventually Occur In My Future?* How will it affect me financially? Socially? Emotionally? Spiritually? In my friendships and family? How will it affect those I love if I refuse to embrace the correction?

4. *What Prevents Me From Making This Change?* Am I willing to live with the limitations and consequences of my stubborn and rebellious decision?

5. *Am I Truly Thankful To God For The Correction?* Or, am I sullen, sulking, and withdrawn?

6. *If It Is Not The Truth, Why Am I Upset?*

3 Tips On Receiving Correction From Those In Authority Over You

1. Ask Them Routinely What Changes They Would Recommend That You Make To Complete Your Daily Tasks.

2. Make Them Your Mentors. Invite them to schedule seminars, create book lists, etc. for you to improve your performance.

3. Refuse To Focus On Their Lack Of Grace In Correcting You. Instead, focus on maximizing and increasing your level of personal excellence.

3 Reminders When Giving Correction To Others

1. *Be Sensitive About The Timing Of Sharing Your Observations With Your Mate Or Members Of Your Family.* When people have

difficult days at the office, patiently wait until the appropriate time to open your heart about making changes.

2. *Firmly, But Gently, Tell Them Your Feelings.* Be careful not to criticize them as individuals, but tell them how their behavior and conduct affected or offended you and why.

3. *Remind Them That You Too Welcome Their Observations And Explanations.*

Success comes naturally to those who are willing to be mentored and corrected.

Some months ago, I saw a revelation in Scripture that intrigued me. I have always been a little shocked that Peter was so outspoken to Jesus. In fact, I have been shocked to see the uncouth, unchecked, and ignorant response of Peter to the foot washing. "Peter said unto Him, Thou shalt never wash my feet" (John 13:8).

Then it dawned on me. Why would a loud-mouthed, brash, and spontaneous fisherman feel so free to express his ignorant and sometimes stupid opinions in the face of Jesus? The answer is obvious. Jesus created a climate so free, relaxed, and nonjudgmental that anyone could say anything he desired in His presence.

Jesus was not nervous around ignorant men.

Jesus was not intimidated by boisterous, brash, and confrontational people.

Jesus permitted those around Him to say absolutely anything that came to their mind, good or bad, wise or stupid.

This enabled Him to quickly discern the level of their information, faith, and maturity. Had He lived defensively, guardedly, and in a constant posture of critical opinion, men would have been more guarded around him. Their true nature would have never surfaced, and effective ministry to them would have been impossible.

It is an interesting situation I observe around me now. There are people on my staff who are very easy to correct. They gladly make instant changes. They take giant steps toward their future.

Others, who are quite defensive, will even burst into tears at the slightest correction. I find myself withdrawing, withholding valuable suggestions from them fearing that they will become fragmented, demoralized, and discouraged if I correct them.

So, I limit their responsibilities. I cannot make many changes in their agenda, nor recommendations to their daily life. They choose their own pace, and mediocre routine, while maintaining a wonderful climate of love. Unfortunately, they will never taste the rewards of maximum greatness, nor experience the hundredfold fruits of prosperity. It is so unfortunate. I see it happen every day of my life.

Correction accelerates promotion, provision, and leadership in your life.

Embrace it.

Cherish it.

And, thank God for the rest of your life that someone loves you enough to risk losing the friendship, in order to help you succeed.

Remember: *Your Success In Your Assignment Depends On Your Ability To Embrace Correction.*

⮾ 13 ⮾

YOUR ASSIGNMENT IS NOT TO EVERYBODY BUT TO SOMEBODY.

⟶⮞●⮜⟵

Everybody Does Not Need You.
But somebody does.

Moses was assigned to the Israelites. He was their Deliverer. "Come now therefore, and I will send thee unto Pharaoh, that thou mayest bring forth my people the children of Israel out of Egypt" (Exodus 3:10).

Aaron was assigned to Moses. He was his personal spokesman to the Israelites. "And the anger of the Lord was kindled against Moses, and He said, Is not Aaron the Levite thy brother? I know that he can speak well. And also, behold, he cometh forth to meet thee: and when he seeth thee, he will be glad in his heart. And thou shalt speak unto him, and put words in his mouth: and I will be with thy mouth, and with his mouth, and will teach you what ye shall do. And he shall be thy spokesman unto the people: and he shall be, even he shall be to thee instead of a mouth, and thou shalt be to him instead of God" (Exodus 4:14-16).

Ruth was assigned to Naomi. Naomi was her mother-in-law. "And Ruth said, Entreat me not to leave thee, or to return from following after thee: for whither thou goest, I will go; and where thou lodgest, I will lodge: thy people shall be my people, and thy God my God: Where thou diest, will I die, and there will I be buried: the Lord do so to me, and more also, if ought but death part thee and me" (Ruth 1:16,17).

Saul was assigned to rule over Israel. "Then Samuel took a vial of oil, and poured it upon his head, and kissed him, and said, Is it not because the Lord hath anointed thee to be captain over his inheritance?" (1 Sam. 10:1).

David was assigned to the Israelites. "And the Lord said unto Samuel, How long wilt thou mourn for Saul, seeing I have rejected him from reigning over Israel? fill thine horn with oil, and go, I will send thee to Jesse the Bethlehemite: for I have provided me a king among his sons" (1 Sam. 16:1).

Jonathan felt assigned to David. "Then Jonathan and David made a covenant, because he loved him as his own soul" (1 Sam. 18:3).

Your Assignment can be to merely one person, like Aaron to Moses.

Your Assignment may be to one *group* of people, like Moses to the Israelites.

But, your Assignment is never to everyone.

21 Keys That Reveal To Whom You Are Assigned

1. *When You Are Assigned To Someone, You Will Feel Their Pain When They Hurt.* Jesus is assigned to us as our Intercessor. "Seeing then that we have a great high priest, that is passed into the

heavens, Jesus the Son of God, let us hold fast our profession. For we have not an high priest which cannot be touched with the feeling of our infirmities; but was in all points tempted like as we are, yet without sin" (Heb. 4:14,15).

2. *When You Are Assigned To Someone, You Will Rejoice When They Rejoice.* "Rejoice with them that do rejoice, and weep with them that weep" (Rom. 12:15).

3. *When You Are Assigned To Someone, Their Needs Matter More Than Your Own Needs.* "Then Esther bade them return Mordecai this answer, Go, gather together all the Jews that are present in Shushan, and fast ye for me, and neither eat nor drink three days, night or day: I also and my maidens will fast likewise; and so will I go in unto the king, which is not according to the law: and if I perish, I perish" (Esther 4:15,16).

4. *When You Are Assigned To Someone, God Will Anoint You With Supernatural Wisdom To Meet Their Needs.* "And Pharaoh said unto Joseph, I have dreamed a dream, and there is none that can interpret it: and I have heard say of thee, that thou canst understand a dream to interpret it. And Joseph said unto Pharaoh, The dream of Pharaoh is one; God hath shewed Pharaoh what He is about to do. And Pharaoh said unto Joseph, Forasmuch as God hath shewed thee all this, there is none so discreet and wise as thou art: Thou shalt be over my house, and according unto thy word shall all my people be ruled: only in the throne will I be greater than thou" (Gen. 41:15,25,39,40).

5. *When You Are Assigned To Someone, You*

Will Possess Uncommon Patience Toward Them. "We give thanks to God always for you all, making mention of you in our prayers; Remembering without ceasing your work of faith, and labour of love, and patience of hope in our Lord Jesus Christ, in the sight of God and our Father" (1 Thess. 1:2,3).

6. *When You Are Assigned To Someone, You Will Leave Your Place Of Comfort To Minister To Them.* "And Ruth said, Entreat me not to leave thee, or to return from following after thee: for whither thou goest, I will go; and where thou lodgest, I will lodge: thy people shall be my people, and thy God my God: Where thou diest, will I die, and there will I be buried: the Lord do so to me, and more also, if aught but death part thee and me" (Ruth 1:16,17).

7. *When You Are Assigned To Someone, Their Enemies Become Your Enemies.* "And David spake to the men that stood by him, saying, What shall be done to the man that killeth this Philistine, and taketh away the reproach from Israel? for who is this uncircumcised Philistine, that he should defy the armies of the living God?" (1 Sam. 17:26).

8. *When You Are Assigned To Someone, Their Friends Become Your Friends.* "And Ruth said, Entreat me not to leave thee, or to return from following after thee: for whither thou goest, I will go; and where thou lodgest, I will lodge: thy people shall be my people, and thy God my God: Where thou diest, will I die, and there will I be buried: the Lord do so to me, and more also, if aught but death part thee and me" (Ruth 1:16,17).

9. *When You Are Assigned To Someone, Their Adversity Becomes Your Own Adversity.* "But

Jonathan Saul's son delighted much in David: and Jonathan told David, saying, Saul my father seeketh to kill thee: now therefore, I pray thee, take heed to thyself until the morning, and abide in a secret place, and hide thyself: And I will go out and stand beside my father in the field where thou art, and I will commune with my father of thee; and what I see, that I will tell thee" (1 Sam. 19:2,3).

10. *When You Are Assigned To Someone, Their Vision Becomes Your Vision.* "Then I told them of the hand of my God which was good upon me; as also the king's words that he had spoken unto me. And they said, Let us rise up and build. So they strengthened their hands for this good work" (Neh. 2:18).

11. *When You Are Assigned To Someone, Their Focus Becomes Your Focus.* It happened to Elisha. "And he left the oxen, and ran after Elijah, and said, Let me, I pray thee, kiss my father and my mother, and then I will follow thee. And he said unto him, Go back again: for what have I done to thee? And he returned back from him, and took a yoke of oxen, and slew them, and boiled their flesh with the instruments of the oxen, and gave unto the people, and they did eat. Then he arose, and went after Elijah, and ministered unto him" (1 Kings 19:20,21).

12. *When You Are Assigned To Someone, You Are Happy Every Time You See Them.* "Is not Aaron the Levite thy brother? I know that he can speak well. And also, behold, he cometh forth to meet thee: and when he seeth thee, he will be glad in his heart" (Exodus 4:14; also see 1 Cor. 16:17,18).

13. *When You Are Assigned To Someone, You*

Are Willing To Give Them That Which Is Valuable To You To Convey Your Loyalty In Covenant. "And Jonathan stripped himself of the robe that was upon him, and gave it to David, and his garments, even to his sword, and to his bow, and to his girdle" (1 Sam. 18:4).

14. *When You Are Assigned To Someone, You Will Risk Alienation From Others You Love To Protect The One To Whom You Are Assigned.* "Then Saul's anger was kindled against Jonathan, and he said unto him, Thou son of the perverse rebellious woman, do not I know that thou hast chosen the son of Jesse to thine own confusion, and unto the confusion of thy mother's nakedness? For as long as the son of Jesse liveth upon the ground, thou shalt not be established, nor thy kingdom. Wherefore now send and fetch him unto me, for he shall surely die. And Jonathan answered Saul his father, and said unto him, Wherefore shall he be slain? what hath he done? And Saul cast a javelin at him to smite him: whereby Jonathan knew that it was determined of his father to slay David" (1 Sam. 20:30-33).

15. *When You Are Assigned To Someone, You Have A Desire To Protect Them.* Jonathan felt this way about David. "And Jonathan said, Far be it from thee: for if I knew certainly that evil were determined by my father to come upon thee, then would not I tell it thee?" (1 Sam. 20:9).

16. *When You Are Assigned To Someone, You Will Plead Their Cause To Their Enemies.* "And Jonathan spake good of David unto Saul his father, and said unto him, Let not the king sin against his servant, against David; because he hath not sinned

against thee, and because his works have been to thee-ward very good" (1 Sam. 19:4).

17. *When You Are Assigned To Someone, You Delight In Their Prosperity.* "Beloved, I wish above all things that thou mayest prosper and be in health, even as thy soul prospereth" (3 John 2). ""Let the Lord be magnified, which hath pleasure in the prosperity of His servant" (Ps. 35:27).

18. *When You Are Assigned To Someone, Their Spiritual Condition Matters.* "And Philip ran thither to him, and heard him read the prophet Esaias, and said, Understandest thou what thou readest? And he said, How can I, except some man should guide me? And he desired Philip that he would come up and sit with him" (Acts 8:30,31).

19. *When You Are Assigned To Someone, You Willingly Expose Hidden Pain.* "For we would not, brethren, have you ignorant of our trouble which came to us in Asia, that we were pressed out of measure, above strength, insomuch that we despaired even of life" (2 Cor. 1:8).

20. *When You Are Assigned To Someone, You Will Risk Personal Loss To Guarantee Their Gain.* "And Jonathan answered Saul his father, and said unto him, Wherefore shall he be slain? what hath he done? And Saul cast a javelin at him to smite him: whereby Jonathan knew that it was determined of his father to slay David" (1 Sam. 20:32,33).

21. *When You Are Assigned To Someone, You Will Feel Uncommon Mercy And Forgiveness Toward Them.* "And he arose, and came to his father. But when he was yet a great way off, his father saw him, and had compassion, and ran, and

fell on his neck, and kissed him" (Luke 15:20).

It is possible to attempt to help too many people. This explains why Paul declared, "but this *one* thing I do" (Phil. 3:13).

J. Paul Getty, the billionaire, once said, "I have seen as many people fail from attempting too many things as those who fail attempting too few."

How do you destroy a man with a great dream? Give him a second one. It will fragment his focus, dilute his energy, and destroy his concentration.

You are not responsible *for* everyone.

You are responsible *to* someone.

Remember: *Your Assignment Is Not To Everybody, But To Somebody.* Find them.

≈ 14 ≈

YOUR ASSIGNMENT MAY BE TO ONLY ONE PERSON WHO WILL HAVE AN IMPACT ON MILLIONS OF OTHERS.

No Assignment Is Small In The Eyes Of God.

Naaman was the captain of the armies of the king of Syria. Scriptures call him "a great man with his master, and honourable, because by him the Lord had given deliverance unto Syria: he was also a mighty man in valour, but he was a leper" (2 Kings 5:1).

Thousands of soldiers obeyed him. He had political clout. His advice and opinions were pursued. The husbands and sons of the entire country obeyed every instruction he gave. The king depended upon his counsel, courage, and brilliant mind.

Unfortunately, he was a leper.

His wife had a maid. Nobody knows her name, even to this very day. The Scriptures did not even record it. She washed, folded, and ironed clothes for a living. She was probably poor. Few sought her advice. Undoubtedly, she worked long hours each day.

But, she had compassion toward Naaman, her boss. She was quite aware of the man of God, Elisha, and the double portion anointing wrapped around his life. She was politically informed, perhaps because of overhearing conversations in the home of the captain. But, most important of all, she was spiritually informed and aware.

She was bold. She was confident. And, she spoke aloud her faith in the man of God. "And she said unto her mistress, Would God my lord were with the prophet that is in Samaria! for he would recover him of his leprosy" (2 Kings 5:3).

Somebody Close To You Can Often Connect You To Someone Who Can Change Your Life.

Naaman came with his horses and his chariot, and stood at the door of the house of Elisha. Elisha sent him a message to go and wash in Jordan river seven times and his leprosy would leave. Though angered by this instruction, Naaman eventually obeyed. "Then went he down, and dipped himself seven times in Jordan, according to the saying of the man of God: and his flesh came again like unto the flesh of a little child, and he was clean" (2 Kings 5:14).

The Assignment of one little housemaid affected others. "And he returned to the man of God, he and all his company, and came, and stood before him: and he said, Behold, now I know that there is no God in all the earth, but in Israel: now therefore, I pray thee, take a blessing of thy servant...for thy servant will henceforth offer neither burnt offering nor sacrifice unto other gods, but unto the Lord" (2 Kings 5:15,17).

▶ The captain of thousands declared a public covenant of commitment to God.

▶ His leaders, and even the ear of the king were now under the influence of a man touched by the hand of God.

▶ *The faith of one maid changed a nation.* "For who hath despised the day of small things?" (Zech. 4:10). "Though thy beginning was small, yet thy latter end should greatly increase" (Job 8:7).

Even Jesus scheduled a visit to a city to have an appointment with just *one* woman. He sensed her need. This woman, who had been married five times, was like a magnet for his anointing. "And He must needs go through Samaria" (John 4:4).

It was there that He began a conversation at Jacob's well. Jesus initiated the conversation. "Give me to drink." None of the disciples were around because they had gone away into the city to buy meat. The woman was shocked. "Then saith the woman of Samaria unto Him, How is it that thou, being a Jew, askest drink of me, which am a woman of Samaria? for the Jews have no dealings with the Samaritans" (John 4:9).

Jesus explained that He would give her water. She would never thirst again. Then, He revealed that He knew she had had five husbands. The woman was spiritually awakened. "The woman then left her waterpot, and went her way into the city, and saith to the men, Come, see a man, which told me all things that ever I did: is not this the Christ?" (John 4:28,29).

One hurting woman was the Golden Connection

to the people of the city. "Then they went out of the city, and came unto Him. So when the Samaritans were come unto Him, they besought Him that He would tarry with them: and He abode there two days. And many more believed because of His own word; And said unto the woman, Now we believe, not because of thy saying: for we have heard Him ourselves, and know that this is indeed the Christ, the Saviour of the world" (John 4:30,40-42).

Oh, my precious friend! Do not belittle any Assignment God has given to you at this time. You may feel that the crowds are applauding others. The glory of God is falling in other places where thousands have gathered. *But, your Assignment is as vital, vibrant, and important as that of any other human on this earth.*

You must believe this *right now*. Embrace it.

Philip went down to the city of Samaria where Jesus had been talking to the woman at the well. Many were saved there. After the crucifixion, Philip was assigned to go there. The Bible says, "And the people with one accord gave heed unto those things which Philip spake, hearing and seeing the miracles which he did. For unclean spirits, crying with loud voice, came out of many that were possessed with them: and many taken with palsies, and that were lame, were healed" (Acts 8:6,7).

This is interesting. Jesus had visited the city.

Many believed Him.

Yet, many *remained* demon-possessed.

The Assignment of Jesus was the *woman*.

The Assignment of Philip was *the possessed*.

▶ *Your Assignment will always bring joy to*

someone. "And there was great joy in that city" (Acts 8:8).

▶ *Your Assignment is always to a place.* In the midst of this tremendous wave of spiritual awakening, "And the angel of the Lord spake unto Philip, saying, Arise, and go toward the south unto the way that goeth down from Jerusalem unto Gaza, which is desert" (Acts 8:26).

▶ *Somebody needs you today and the Holy Spirit knows exactly where he or she is located.* "And he arose and went: and, behold, a man of Ethiopia, an eunuch of great authority under Candace queen of the Ethiopians, who had the charge of all her treasure, and had come to Jerusalem for to worship, Was returning, and sitting in his chariot read Esaias the prophet" (Acts 8:27,28).

▶ *The Holy Spirit knows to whom you are assigned.* "Then the Spirit said unto Philip, Go near, and join thyself to this chariot" (Acts 8:29). He knows where they live. He knows the questions you can answer in their lives. You are a walking reward to those people.

Philip ran to him. He explained the gospel. Then he baptized the Ethiopian, "And when they were come up out of the water, the Spirit of the Lord caught away Philip, that the eunuch saw him no more: and he went on his way rejoicing" (Acts 8:39).

According to some historians, 90 percent of Ethiopia came to Christ through the testimony of this eunuch. The Holy Spirit spoke to *one man*, Philip, to go meet *another man* in the desert. Revival broke out, and *thousands* came to Christ.

Do not despise what appears to be a trivial Assignment. Nothing is small to God—absolutely nothing. If He made it, it is important to Him.

Whatever your present Assignment may be, cultivate *excellence* in it. Do it right. Do the best you can at this time. Abandon yourself to *completing* it.

Something bigger than you have ever imagined is on the other side of this Assignment.

Remember: *Your Assignment May Be To Only One Person Who Will Have An Impact On Millions Of Others.*

≈ 15 ≈

GRATITUDE IS OFTEN A CONFIRMATION OF YOUR ASSIGNMENT.

Any Drowning Man Appreciates A Life Jacket.
Many need you.
Few appreciate you.

Those few, to whom you have been assigned, will confirm it through their respect and appreciation of you.

This explains the instructions of Jesus to His disciples. "And into whatsoever city or town ye shall enter, inquire who in it is worthy; and there abide till ye go thence. And when ye come into an house, salute it. And if the house be worthy, let your peace come upon it: but if it be not worthy, let your peace return to you. And whosoever shall not receive you, nor hear your words, when ye depart out of that house or city, shake off the dust of your feet" (Matt. 10:11-14).

Many people needed miracles in the days of Jesus. Why did He stop for a blind man sitting by the highway begging? Jesus had a schedule. He had appointments. He had His disciples and a great number of people around Him.

The blind man discerned His value.

The responsiveness of the blind man attracted Jesus. "And many charged him that he should hold his peace; but he cried the more a great deal, Thou son of David, have mercy on me. And Jesus stood still, and commanded him to be called. And they call the blind man, saying unto him, Be of good comfort, rise; he calleth thee" (Mark 10:48,49).

The woman with the issue of blood appreciated Jesus. She had suffered for 12 years. The Bible said she had suffered "many things of many physicians." She had spent every cent she had. She had never improved. In fact, the Bible says she "grew worse" (read Mark 5:25,26).

When she heard of Jesus, she pressed in behind Him and touched His garment. Listen to her incredible faith, her confidence in Jesus, and her appreciation. "For she said, If I may touch but His clothes, I shall be whole. And straightway the fountain of her blood was dried up; and she felt in her body that she was healed of that plague" (Mark 5:28,29).

▶ Who is *responsive* to your presence?
▶ Who *celebrates* every word you speak?
▶ Who responds *swiftly* to your instruction?
▶ Who prefers your presence to all others?
▶ Who is reluctant to leave your side?

Clues are plentiful. Note them.

Remember: *Gratitude Is Often A Confirmation Of Your Assignment.*

∾ 16 ∾

THE ONE WHOSE SUCCESS MATTERS TO YOU THE MOST IS THE ONE TO WHOM YOU ARE ASSIGNED.

———➤●←———

Somebody's Success Should Be Your Obsession.
Who is it? Whose success stays on your mind *all the time?* What person or group of people consume your thoughts?

This is a clue to whom you have been assigned.

God has you on His mind all the time. Listen to David. He is well aware of the love of God toward him. "How precious also are Thy thoughts unto me, O God! how great is the sum of them! If I should count them, they are more in number than the sand: when I awake, I am still with Thee" (Ps. 139:17,18). God sees you as His Assignment. You are on His mind every moment of the day!

God has even assigned angels to you. "But to which of the angels said He at any time, Sit on My right hand, until I make thine enemies thy footstool? Are they not all ministering spirits, sent forth to minister for them who shall be heirs of salvation?" (Heb. 1:13,14).

Those whose success matters to you the most are

those to whom you have been assigned.

A father watches silently as the young lady receives the crown at a national beauty pageant on television. He sips his tea. Then, he calmly walks to the kitchen to eat supper. But, when his daughter calls and says, "Daddy, I got a raise on my job!" He beams. He smiles. He tells all his friends at work that his daughter got a promotion. *She is his Assignment.*

Parents are assigned to their children.

Here is a powerful and important self-test: When a child comes home from school shouting and thrilled over something wonderful occurring in their life, you should feel great joy. If you do not, it is a signal that your focus is not on your Assignment. This must be corrected. If you are more excited over the success of a neighbor than that of your own children, you have failed to acknowledge and discover the center of your own calling.

Thousands of children are being damaged because parents have not embraced their personal Assignment. What can you do? Talk to the Holy Spirit. Confess that something within you has been broken. Your heart needs mending again. Your mind needs renewing. It may be damaged through strife and difficult seasons. Perhaps, your own parents neglected you, and you do not know how to reach out and strengthen your family. Stay teachable. The healing can begin this very moment, even while you are reading this book.

It is possible that satan will use a bitter experience to break your focus and derail you. Only in the presence of the Holy Spirit can that be revealed to you. Only with a humble heart will you be able to make the appropriate changes and bring great joy again to your life.

The Apostle Paul received joy at the victories of others. "For ye are our glory and joy" (1 Thess. 2:20). So, note those whose triumphs and victories bring you joy.

Remember: *The One Whose Success Matters To You The Most Is The One To Whom Are You Assigned.*

When God
Wants To Bless You
He Brings A Person
Into Your Life.

-MIKE MURDOCK

❧ 17 ❧

GOD IS CONSTANTLY SCHEDULING GOLDEN CONNECTIONS TO ADVANCE YOUR ASSIGNMENT.

God Can Link You With Anyone Within 24 Hours.

Never forget this. God knows *exactly* where you live. He is fully aware of every human on this planet. Look at the life of Ruth. She went from the peasant fields of Boaz to being his wife in a single day.

Golden Connections are those people who become Divine Bridges that enable you to exit from one season and enter into the next Season of Blessing. The butler was a connection for Joseph to personally meet Pharaoh and interpret his dream.

No relationship is insignificant in your life.

God Is Committed To The Completion Of Your Assignment. "The Lord will perfect that which concerneth me" (Ps. 138:8). "Being confident of this very thing, that He which hath begun a good work in you will perform it until the day of Jesus Christ" (Phil. 1:6).

13 Wisdom Keys You Should Know About The Golden Connection Of Your Life:

1. *You Cannot Succeed Without Golden Connections.* Your Creator planned it. He wanted you to know others. "And the eye cannot say unto the hand, I have no need of thee: nor again the head to the feet, I have no need of you" (1 Cor. 12:21).

There is an interesting Scripture from the Apostle Paul. He describes how each of us fit together. "From whom the whole body fitly joined together and compacted by that which every joint supplieth, according to the effectual working in the measure of every part, maketh increase of the body unto the edifying of itself in love" (Eph. 4:16). Relationships increase us. Multiply us.

2. *When God Wants To Bless You, He Brings A Person Into Your Life.* Look for them. Expect them. Discern them. Be swift to respond to them. "Two are better than one; because they have a good reward for their labour" (Ecc. 4:9).

3. *Your Golden Connection May Not Be Outwardly Appealing.* God uses burlap bags sometimes to carry His Gold Bars of Blessing. The camels of Abraham were not appealing, but they carried the wealth of the patriarch. When Rebecca agreed to water the camels, she connected with Isaac, her wealthy husband-to-be.

Ruth was a Moabite girl, a heathen. But she was Boaz's connection to the lineage of Jesus. Jephthah, a great leader, was thrust out by his family. Jephthah was the son of a harlot. But he was the Golden Connection that brought deliverance to the people of God.

4.   *Do Not Reject A Golden Connection Because It Does Not Meet Your Qualifications For An Intimate Relationship.* Let me explain. The butler may not have been received by Joseph to be a best friend. But he was The Golden Connection to the throne. The Apostle Paul did not want to be shipwrecked on the island of Melita. But God used it as a Divine Connection with the leader of the island, Publius. His father was healed through Paul's ministry. These were Divine and Golden Connections that had been scheduled by God.

5.   *Crisis Always Brings Good People To- gether.* Expect to find gold in every fiery furnace of your life. Best friends often come together through disasters and tragedies. Many times I have heard the remark, "This is my best friend. We met during a crisis."

Some time ago I read some statistics on relationships. According to the report, you are just four people away from any human on earth. This means that *you* know someone...who knows *another* person...who knows a third person...who is connected to *anyone you could possibly meet* on earth. This includes leaders of nations and CEOs of corporations. God can get anyone to you anywhere you are.

6.   *Recognize That God Often Uses Illogical Methods And Unlikely People To Help Fulfill Your Assignment.* I have often said that if you can figure something out, God is probably not in it. God is a supernatural, miracle working God.

Picture the Ethiopian eunuch. He is puzzled and bewildered. He desperately needs a Divine

Connection with the man of God. "Then the Spirit said unto Philip, Go near, and join thyself to this chariot. And Philip ran thither to him" (Acts 8:29,30). Yes, God can get The Golden Connection to you within 24 hours.

7. The *Golden Connection* Is Not Necessarily Your Best Friend. As you recall, the butler forgot Joseph for two years after his exit from the prison!

8. The *Golden Connection* May Not Necessarily Feel Loyal To You. The Connection may not even consider you essential or even desirable.

9. The *Golden Connection* For Your Life May Have Flaws Repulsive To You. Yet, God will use their difference or gift...to bless you.

10. The *Golden Connection* May Not Be A Mentor Nor A Protégé.

11. The *Golden Connection* May Depart From Your Life, Never To Be Seen Again After God Uses Them.

12. The *Golden Connection* May Be Used By The Holy Spirit To Move You From A Place Of Loss To A Place Of Favor.

13. *Someone Is Always Observing You Today Who Is Capable Of Greatly Blessing You Tomorrow.* Remember Ruth. Boaz was discussing her with his employees weeks before she even knew he noticed her. Somebody is discussing your promotion this very moment. Somewhere in the seat of power and decision-making, your name is being considered. Get your faith up! Sow Seeds of Expectation every day!

God is planning something so big that no devil can stop it—The Golden Connection.

Remember: *God Is Constantly Scheduling Golden Connections To Advance Your Assignment.*

⇜ 18 ⇝

YOUR PRESENT ASSIGNMENT MAY MERELY BE A BRIDGE TO A GREATER SEASON.

Your Present Situation Is Probably Temporary.
Joseph stayed aware of this at all times. It preserved his mind. It kept Him focused. He never accepted his present trial as a permanent place. That is why he told the butler returning to the palace, "But think on me when it shall be well with thee, and show kindness, I pray thee, unto me, and make mention of me unto Pharaoh, *and bring me out of this house*" (Gen. 40:14).

Naomi was an Assignment for Ruth. However, Naomi was The Golden Connection to Ruth's husband, Boaz (see Ruth 1-4).

Never despise where God has placed you. He has a master plan and blueprint for your life. It is a *wise* plan. It will *benefit* you. Your present season is merely a Bridge, a Connection, a Gate to something so wonderful He cannot even tell you all the details yet.

It is tempting to become agitated when the benefits of the present season seem exhausted. It was this sin that robbed the Israelites from their reward of Canaan.

They complained in Egypt.

Then, they complained in the wilderness.

They complained continuously.

Golden Connections are created ahead of time. You must believe that God has scheduled your present situation. It contains purpose and benefit. You must determine to stay there long enough for Him to complete His Assignment.

You must exhaust the benefits of your present before God will promote you into your next season.

You may never pass this way again.

Take a sheet of paper and draw up an inventory of your present season: the *benefits* of your present circumstances. Do not yet create a list of the disadvantages, pain, and lack of benefits. Rather, make a detailed inventory of what God has *presently* provided for your life.

What complimentary or free benefits do you receive? Who are the people you have access to today who possess something you need, desire, or respect? What knowledge is close to you that you have not yet pursued? What currents of favor are presently flowing toward your life from others?

Drop your bucket in the Well of the Present and draw out water continuously. As I told a young travel assistant once, "Son, I am paying your airline tickets to fly all across the world. I am paying for your hotel bills, your food bills, luggage, and clothing. You are being introduced to the highest caliber of humans known on earth. You are permitted to sit in the counsel of brilliant people. Every single day of your life, you hear the teaching of a proven man of God. You eat the greatest food ever cooked on earth in the finest restaurants possible. You may never pass this way again. Stop complaining about long hours, and inventory the benefits of the present season that may never occur again the rest of your life."

Are you going through a difficult season? Have you developed bitterness? Anger? Cynicism? These must be burned out of your heart by the presence of the Holy Spirit. Move toward Him today.

Is your present season a battle? Extract every possible benefit from it.

Bad times bring good people together. It was in the *starvation* season that the widow of Zarephath connected with the greatest man of *faith* in her generation. It was during false accusation that Joseph met the butler, the confidant of Pharaoh who made him Prime Minister. It was while Ruth was gleaning in fields and gathering barley for a widowed mother-in-law, that she was observed by Boaz, the wealthy man of her city, who eventually married her.

Your Greatest Relationships Are Often Birthed In The Darkest Seasons Of Your Life. When Saul reacted badly toward David, the heart of Jonathan was knit with him. Their friendship was the golden example of what God intended for humans to experience. So, when things are going worse than ever in your life, the most incredible relationships are near and ready to enter.

Your present season will pass. "Behold, I will do a new thing; now it shall spring forth; shall ye not know it? I will even make a way in the wilderness, and rivers in the desert" (Isa. 43:19).

Your present season may seem like the fiery furnace of the three Hebrew children.

You will pass *through* this season.

You will pass through your present darkness.

You will move on to the next season of *increased provision and blessing*. "Fear not: for I have redeemed thee, I have called thee by thy name; thou art Mine. When thou passest through the waters, I will be with thee; and through the rivers, they shall not overflow thee: when thou walkest through the fire, thou shalt not be burned; neither shall the flame kindle upon thee" (Isa. 43:1,2). "Whereas ye know not what shall be on the morrow. For what is your life? It is even a vapour, that appeareth for a little time, and then vanisheth away" (James 4:14).

Remember: *Your Present Assignment May Merely Be A Bridge To A Greater Season.*

❧ 19 ❧

EACH MOMENT IS AN OPPORTUNITY TO ADVANCE IN YOUR ASSIGNMENT.

One Moment Can Make A Difference.
Time is *so* precious. It is impossible to save, store, or gather Time. You must simply learn the best ways to invest it.

Moments really do matter. The Apostle Paul treasured time. "See then that ye walk circumspectly, not as fools, but as wise, Redeeming the time, because the days are evil" (Eph. 5:15,16).

Time is the currency of earth. Mexico has the peso. France has the franc. Germany has the mark. The United States has the dollar. God has given a currency to us here on earth—the currency called Time.

Think about this. God did not simply give you friends. He gave you *Time.* You accepted Time and invested Time back into people. That produced friendships. God did not simply give you money. He gave you *Time.* You offered your Time to an employer and traded your Time for his money. You took the money and purchased your home.

Time is one of the most precious and valuable gifts God has given to you.

Study the success habits of uncommon achievers. You will notice one obvious and outstanding quality. All champions and leaders are very conscious of time. They wear watches. They continually consult them. When you have an appointment with them, they establish the perimeters of the appointment. Boundaries are set. You simply do not meet someone at 3:00 p.m. You will meet with them from 3:00 p.m. until 3:30 p.m.

Why is this? Their Time is the most precious commodity in their life. It is the currency of time that helps them strengthen their families, birth ideas, and achieve their dreams and goals.

I must make something very clear to you if I am to help you achieve your Assignment. There are people who are poor by the standards of today. Many of those who are struggling have a common thread —an obvious disrespect for time.

They are late for appointments.

They do not have a written plan for each day.

Conversations are vague instead of focused.

Your Respect For Time Is A Prediction Of Your Financial Future. I read an interesting illustration many years ago. If you have five pounds of iron, you can use it three different ways:

1) It can be used to make *horseshoes*. If so, it would be worth approximately $10.

2) You can use the five pounds of iron to make *needles*. In this form, it would be worth approximately $300.

3) You can use the iron to make *watch springs*. In that form, it would be worth thousands of dollars. The same amount of iron, used three different ways, will produce three different levels of financial income.

Your time is much like this bar of iron. You can watch a television movie for two hours. Or, you can read and absorb the financial success secrets from the biography of a billionaire. You can sit at your table and eat a meal for ninety minutes and talk with your friends. Or, you can eat for 30 minutes and go walk four miles in the following 60 minutes. You decide.

▶ *Champions Make Decisions That Create The Future They Desire.*

▶ *Losers Make Decisions That Create The Present They Desire.*

You must cultivate a total focus on your Assignment. Remember, you will only succeed with something that is an obsession. Last night, I was readying the biography of the fascinating entrepreneur of our generation, the late Sam Walton, head of the Wal-Mart stores. Throughout the book, he continuously referred to the fact that he was obsessed with retailing.

He spent *every available moment* studying retail sales.

Those moments paid off.

7 Keys In Making Moments Count

1. *Keep A Calendar Or Day Planner With You At All Times.* What You See Determines What You Desire. Someone has well said, "A short pencil is better than a long memory." God instructed us, "Write the vision, and make it plain upon tables, that he may run that readeth it" (Hab. 2:2).

Your day planner should be handy and kept with you always. If it is too large, you will use its size as an excuse to leave it at home, or in the car. At first, carrying *anything* will become uncomfortable. However, remember that it is your blueprint for the dreams and goals of your life. Others may sit around and discuss the weather, the wind or current news.

You are on an Assignment.

You are focused.

2. *Stay Aware Of Each Hour As It Occurs.* Develop precision with each appointment. "For the vision is yet for an appointed time, but at the end it shall speak, and not lie: though it tarry, wait for it; because it will surely come, it will not tarry" (Hab. 2:3).

3. *Review The Appointments And Plans Of Each Day Continually.* Visualize them as links to your eventual goal and dream.

4. *Read Continuously.* When I am in an airplane, waiting at the airport or sitting in a taxi, I *read.* I read newspapers, magazines, books, or my Bible. I try to absorb everything related to my Assignment. Occasionally, I will read a novel for relaxation. When I do, I have a pen in hand to circle anything in that novel linked to something I want to do with my life.

Extract an education from events, people, and reading material around you. *Cultivate* that kind of appetite, even if you are not born with it.

Clip articles out of newspapers. Tear pages out of magazines, and build files—anything to strengthen your resolve and focus on the Assignment God is burning into your life.

5. *Listen. Listen. Listen.* While listening, ask questions. When you are with a lawyer, ask him

which three most important things he feels you should know. When you are visiting a Realtor, ask him the three most important characteristics of buying and selling a home. When you are with your pastor, ask him the three most important daily habits necessary for birthing a powerful, relationship with God.

6. *Ask Questions That Control The Focus And Quality Of Every Conversation.* Keep a legal pad and a pen or a microcassette with you at all times. There is probably never a moment I do not have a micro cassette in my hand or pocket, or a legal pad. Why? *One idea could birth a million miracles.*

I have a very special friend who is quite successful. Every word that comes forth from his lips is like gold. In his presence, I am rejuvenated and invigorated, and I become quite imaginative. When he talks, things happen within me. It is like fireworks going off. When I am in his presence, time does not matter. Why? He gives me something I cannot get anywhere else. So, I keep my recorder and paper busy every time we are together.

I cannot afford to waste a minute of my time doing something unrelated to my Assignment. You, too, must make every moment count in your life.

7. *Enter Into Conversations That Advance Your Assignment.* Keep focused. Occasionally, I have people approach me and want to talk about things unrelated to my calling. I simply refuse. Why? I am ruthless in protecting my focus on the Assignment God has placed in my life.

Someone called my office a few weeks back. "Hello, Mike! I want to discuss a business proposition with you!"

"Does it have anything to do with the Wisdom of God?" I asked.

"Not really, but I am loving it, and want to sit down for a day and share it with you."

"I am sorry, but my present Assignment from God is taking up 24 hours a day, seven days a week, and 365 days a year. When I feel His Assignment changing in me, I will telephone you!" I graciously hung up.

If I returned every telephone call, answered every single question asked of me, flew to every city where someone had requested me, listened to every cassette mailed to me, or read every book handed to me, I would not have time to live one single day of my life properly.

Every moment is valuable. You have nothing to give to those who disrespect your time.

Access to God was His first gift to you.

Time was His *second* gift to you.

Do not squander it in any way. It is the precious gift of time that enables you to enter into The Secret Place, read the Word of God, and do what He has assigned you to do.

When a young lady met me at a restaurant for our date, she was 45 minutes late. She laughed it off. I could hardly believe how lightly she considered time. Obviously, the relationship did not work out.

Your respect for time will always distance you from others.

Disconnect from people who do not appreciate your time. Several years ago, I flew 1,500 miles to a crusade. It was a Saturday evening. I was speaking Sunday, both morning and night. Then, I would fly back home Monday afternoon. It involved three days of my life in a strange motel room, away from my home and family. The pastor leaned over to me Sunday night and whispered, "Could you get us out within 40 minutes?"

"I can get you out right now," I replied. "If you have flown me here 3,000 miles for three days and do not desire more than 40 minutes of Wisdom, I am in the wrong place anyway." I have refused to return to that church.

When you see somebody who is flippant and careless with their time, know they will be flippant and careless with your time as well. I have seen people come and sit around my offices and ministry doing very little, then ask me for a job. If they are careless with their own hours, imagine what they would do working for me.

I replied to a resume once. Nobody answered the telephone. I was surprised that an answering machine did not accommodate me. When I finally talked to the job applicant, I asked, "Why do you not have a telephone answering machine?"

"I do not like answering machines," was her reply.

Obviously, I would not even consider hiring someone who was that insensitive to time. What did that tell me? Her friends' time did not matter. She forced everyone to keep returning phone calls to reach her. When someone telephoned her, they were unable to leave any messages. Consequently, they wasted their entire effort, time, energy, and finances. I could not afford to have someone so thoughtless on my payroll.

I would be reluctant to hire anyone who wrote me long 15 page letters. Why? Their time does not matter. They refuse conciseness. They force their friends to read trivia and absorb nonessential information—simply because they do not want to think before writing.

I have sat for several hours in the presence of young preachers who are launching their ministries. Few have ever asked me one serious, thoughtful, and important question. Oh, how we waste the time God has given to us! Time is a wonderful and glorious tool God has given you to build your dream, your goals, and your Assignment. Do not throw it away.

"To every thing there is a season, and a time to every purpose under the heaven: A time to be born, and a time to die; a time to plant, and a time to pluck up that which is planted; A time to kill, and a time to heal; a time to break down, and a time to build up; A time to weep, and a time to laugh; a time to mourn, and a time to dance; A time to cast away stones, and a time to gather stones together; a time to embrace, and a time to refrain from embracing; A time to get, and a time to lose; a time to keep, and a time to cast away; A time to rend, and a time to sew; a time to keep silence, and a time to speak; A time to love, and a time to hate; a time of war, and a time of peace" (Ecc. 3:1-8).

Remember: *Each Moment Is An Opportunity To Advance In Your Assignment.*

≈ 20 ≈

YOUR ASSIGNMENT IS ACTUALLY AN HOURLY EVENT.

Maximize Today.

Yesterday is already over, so it really does not exist anymore. It is in the past. It is over. It is in the tomb. Tomorrow is in the womb. It has not been born yet. It is not here. It really is not your life because you have not seen it yet.

Your life is today.

This may sound a little strange, but you really will never *see* the future. Ever. When you arrive in your future, you will rename it "today."

Three years ago, you may have made a declaration, "In three years, I will be doing such and such." Well, you are here. This is three years later. Yet, what are you doing *today*? Are you still talking about your *future*? Are you still talking about what you will do five years from now? You will never get there. Never.

When you get into your future, you will re-name it "today."

The Key to Life is discerning the essentials of The Perfect Day, and making it happen habitually.

The Perfect Day

Several years ago, the Lord gave me an interesting picture while I was on a fast. I saw my life as a Golden Train on the Track of Success. In my "future", I saw Cities of Achievement along the track. My Golden Train of Life was racing toward those Cities of Achievement.

I saw 24 Golden Box Cars being pulled by me each morning. Every morning, God gives you 24 Golden Hours. What you place in each of those 24 Golden Box Cars determines the speed and the distance your Train will move toward those next Cities of Achievement.

I noticed that I would often allow someone to come and sit in my office and "kill my time." They simply had nothing to do. I tried to be courteous and friendly by working quietly around them. Yet, they were filling up my hours with their idleness. My Golden Train was slowing down in the process.

If you do not decide the cargo of each of the 24 Golden Box Cars of each day, somebody else will decide the cargo and overload them. If someone else overloads your cars, your Golden Train will derail. Progress becomes impossible.

An Unproductive Day Is Always An Unhappy Day. You were created for increase. It is natural to increase and unnatural to decrease. So, every day you receive from God a fresh beginning. You can begin your life all over again.

Today is a "*mini*-life." It is a small, prototype of your *lifetime*.

If you failed today, do not get discouraged. Review it. Analyze it. What *missing* ingredients are obvious? What ingredients must be *added?* If you do not know the essential ingredients of a Perfect Day, you will never know the ingredients of a wonderful and glorious lifetime.

When a famous hamburger chain discovered how to make their store successful, they *duplicated* it. They made it happen hundreds of times throughout the earth. They did not begin *multiplying* until they had created a perfect store, a *prototype* of what they wanted to *multiply*.

Most of us have never discovered how to carefully sculpture even one wonderful and glorious day...The Perfect Day. "But the path of the just is as the shining light, that shineth more and more unto the perfect day" (Prov. 4:18).

Your life should have a daily plan. "For which of you, intending to build a tower, sitteth not down first, and counteth the cost, whether he have sufficient to finish it? Lest haply, after he hath laid the foundation, and is not able to finish it, all that behold it begin to mock him, Saying, This man began to build, and was not able to finish" (Luke 14:28-30).

Nobody really knows your future except your Father. The Apostle Paul himself said, "And now, behold, I go bound in the spirit unto Jerusalem, not knowing the things that shall befall me there: Save that the Holy Ghost witnesseth in every city, saying that bonds and afflictions abide me" (Acts 20:22,23).

You must become time-conscious in spiritual matters. "To day if ye will hear His voice, harden not your hearts" (Heb. 4:7).

You must encourage your love circle daily. These are those who are closest to you. "But exhort one another daily, while it is called Today; lest any of you be hardened through the deceitfulness of sin" (Heb. 3:13).

One Discovery Can Birth A Lifetime Of Prosperity. Each day is a chance to create a perfect life. Your life *is* today. Every morning you will receive another opportunity to create The Perfect Day.

Your provision is a daily event. Jesus prayed this prayer, "Give us day by day our daily bread" (Luke 11:3).

You should mentor someone daily. Jesus did. "And He taught daily in the temple" (Luke 19:47).

You must daily pursue and accept mercy and forgiveness for any wrong. "It is of the Lord's mercies that we are not consumed, because His compassions fail not. They are new every morning: great is Thy faithfulness" (Lam. 3:22,23).

Eternity is in you. You were created a pilgrim. You are on a journey. It never ends. You see, He is our Alpha and Omega, the beginning and the end. "Looking unto Jesus, the Author and Finisher of our faith" (Heb. 12:2). "For in Him we live, and move, and have our being" (Acts 17:28).

You were created for movement. You are constantly moving toward Him, toward your Assignment, toward the dreams and goals He has planned for your life. Will you *arrive?*

Only when He is your destination.

Remember: *Your Assignment Is Actually An Hourly Event.*

❧ 21 ❧

YOUR WILLINGNESS, NOT YOUR PERFECTION, WILL QUALIFY YOU FOR YOUR ASSIGNMENT.

———————

Your Flaws Will Not Necessarily Disqualify You.
Your *attitude* can.

Your Assignment is perfect.

You are not. "For He knoweth our frame; He remembereth that we are dust" (Ps. 103:14).

Your goodness is not enough to qualify you for your Assignment. I wrote a song many years ago, "He Does Not Always Call The Qualified, But He Qualifies The Called." The Scripture says, "But we are all as an unclean thing, and all our righteousnesses are as filthy rags; and we all do fade as a leaf; and our iniquities, like the wind, have taken us away" (Isa. 64:6).

The psalmist declared, "every man at his best state is altogether vanity" (Ps. 39:5).

Review the Heroes of Faith in Hebrews 11. Why are they celebrated? None of them are remembered for their lives of perfection, but rather for their *confidence* toward God. Their *faith* was magnetic and powerful.

They were *willing* to do anything God said.

Abraham lied. Twice! He told his wife, Sarai, "Say, I pray thee, thou art my sister: that it may be well with me for thy sake; and my soul shall live because of thee" (Gen. 12:13). "And Abraham said of Sarah his wife, She is my sister: and Abimelech king of Gerar sent, and took Sarah" (Gen. 20:2). Obviously, it was not his lifestyle nor pattern of life, but fear affected his integrity.

Jacob lied. He deceived his father, Isaac, to secure the birthright from his older brother, Esau. His mother, Rebecca, cooperated with him. "And Jacob said unto his father, I am Esau thy firstborn; I have done according as thou badest me: arise, I pray thee, sit and eat of my venison, that thy soul may bless me" (Gen. 27:19). His sons then followed his habit of deception.

The sons of Jacob lied. What Jacob made happen for his father, his sons made happen for him in deceiving him regarding Joseph. Yet, Jacob continued to pursue God so intensely that God even changed his name!

Moses was a murderer. He became a fugitive from the law. He killed an Egyptian whom he saw beating a Hebrew worker. Fearful, he ran away to hide in the desert. His life was scarred, marred, and alienated from the very place where he was supposed to be a Deliverer (see Exodus 2:11-15). Yet, we see that God did not forget him. The angel appeared to him in a burning bush. God spoke to Moses and reminded him of his Assignment.

Your *worthiness* does not qualify you.

Your *willingness* to heal qualifies you.

Your abilities do not compel God to use you.

It is God's compassion toward those who need you. "And the Lord said, I have surely seen the affliction of my people which are in Egypt, and have heard their cry by reason of their taskmasters; for I know their sorrows; And I am come down to deliver them out of the hand of the Egyptians, and to bring them up out of that land unto a good land and a large, unto a land flowing with milk and honey" (Exodus 3:7,8).

The pain of the captives causes God to give us an Assignment. The meekness and deep caring heart of Moses made him great. And this man, who was so stained by failure, became a close friend to God. "And the Lord spake unto Moses face to face, as a man speaketh unto his friend" (Exodus 33:11).

Samson visited harlots. He was often vulnerable and weak in the presence of alluring women. "Then went Samson to Gaza, and saw there an harlot, and went in unto her" (Judges 16:1). Yet, his ability to reach for God after failure qualified him to be among the Heroes of Faith in Hebrews (see Heb. 11:32).

When satan has made a fool of you, repentance can create an exit from your failure.

David committed adultery. Then, he murdered Bathsheba's husband, Uriah, to cover up his sin. Yet, the hand of God reached down again and brought healing and forgiveness. Yes, he paid the price. Judgment came. But his *willingness* to get up after failure qualified him to continue with his Assignment (read 2 Sam. 11).

Peter, the blustering fisherman, denied the Lord three times. When pressure came, he folded. "Then began he to curse and to swear, saying, I know not the man. And immediately the cock crew. And Peter remembered the word of Jesus, which said unto him, Before the cock crow, thou shalt deny Me thrice. And he went out, and wept bitterly" (Matt. 26:74,75). Those tears were the river that rushed him toward mercy and restoration.

Peter became so victorious through the mercy of Jesus that he was able to write later, "Wherein ye greatly rejoice, though now for a season, if need be, ye are in heaviness through manifold temptations: That the trial of your faith, being much more precious than of gold that perisheth, though it be tried with fire, might be found unto praise and honour and glory at the appearing of Jesus Christ: Whom having not seen, ye love; in Whom, though now ye see Him not, yet believing, ye rejoice with joy unspeakable and full of glory: Receiving the end of your faith, even the salvation of your souls" (1 Peter 1:6-9).

Have you failed God?

Have you failed those who love you?

Have you felt sick at heart because your conduct and behavior have been unbecoming to a child of God?

Do not quit. Do not stop reaching. Everything you have ever wanted is ahead of you, not behind you.

I wrote a song several years ago, "God's Not Through Blessing You." Here are some of those words:

A man one day lost every dime to his name;
His best friends even said he was through;

God said to Job, your best days are just ahead;
'Cause I am not through blessing you.

God's not through blessing you;
God's not through blessing you;
Never give up, what He said He will do;
God's not through blessing you.

God is not through using you either.

Isaiah 1:19 declares, "If ye be willing and obedient, ye shall eat the good of the land." Believe it.

Remember: *Your Willingness, Not Your Perfection, Will Qualify You For Your Assignment.*

You Will Never Possess
What You Are Unwilling
To Pursue.

-MIKE MURDOCK

❧ 22 ❧

YOUR INVESTMENT IN WISDOM REVEALS YOUR PASSION FOR YOUR ASSIGNMENT.

The Proof Of Desire Is Pursuit.

Wisdom is the greatest gift you can pursue.

It is the secret to uncommon achievement and uncommon greatness.

The Successful value the discoveries of others. I am always amused by those who declare, "there is no new thing under the sun" (Ecc. 1:9). They are quoting a discouraged and disappointed man who pursued materialistic things during apostate seasons of his life.

Solomon did not exhaust the creativity of God on earth. When God rested on the seventh day, He did not stop having ideas and plans. He merely rested. After all, He is the One who promised, "Behold, I will do a new thing; now it shall spring forth; shall ye not know it? I will even make a way in the wilderness, and rivers in the desert" (Isa. 43:19).

His mercies are even described as, "new every morning" (Lam. 3:22).

You are not born with all the Wisdom necessary for your Assignment. Others possess rare and unique gifts and revelations. Paul understood this. "For to one is given by the Spirit the word of Wisdom; to another the word of knowledge by the same Spirit... For as the body is one, and hath many members, and all the members of that one body, being many, are one body: so also is Christ" (1 Cor. 12:8-12).

You need *others.*

You need their *knowledge.*

You need what God has *revealed* to them. "And the eye cannot say unto the hand, I have no need of thee: nor again the head to the feet, I have no need of you" (1 Cor. 12:21).

8 Facts You Should Know About Wisdom

1. *Wisdom Is The Most Important Thing On Earth.* "Wisdom is the principal thing" (Prov. 4:7).

2. *You Must Pursue Wisdom.* It will not come to you. "Get Wisdom, get understanding" (Prov. 4:5).

3. *Wisdom Can Be Forgotten.* You must constantly read and study to keep yourself stirred and reminded. "...forget it not; neither decline from the words of my mouth" (Prov. 4:5).

4. *You Can Know Wisdom And Deliberately Walk Away From It.* "Forsake her not" (Prov. 4:6).

5. *Wisdom Will Preserve And Protect You If You Love And Pursue Her.* "She shall preserve thee: love her, and she shall keep thee" (Prov. 4:6).

6. *Wisdom Is The Key To Every Promotion In Your Life.* "Exalt her, and she shall promote thee" (Prov. 4:8).

7. *Wisdom Brings You Honor, Credibility,*

And Acceptance By Others. "She shall bring thee to honour, when thou dost embrace her. She shall give to thine head an ornament of grace: a crown of glory shall she deliver to thee" (Prov. 4:8,9).

8. *The Wisdom Imparted By God To Men Has Been Documented In Thousands Of Books.* It is accessible, reachable, and just moments away. Think about it: You are reading this book today. Truths burned into my heart late at night in The Secret Place are now beginning to burn in your own heart, too. This is the power of a book. As I have often said, *God sent His Son, but He left His book.*

Books are feared by tyrants. One book can strip the power from a controlling dictator of a country. You have heard in this generation how a novel so incensed an entire nation that a price of millions of dollars was placed on the author's head. Why kill an author? His revelation, opinion or words potentially could strip leaders of their tyrannical power.

4 Facts About Reading

1. *The Most Uncommon Mentor To Ministers, Paul, Urged Personal Reading And Study.* "Study to show thyself approved unto God, a workman that needeth not to be ashamed, rightly dividing the Word of truth" (2 Tim. 2:15).

2. *Reading Wisdom Books Will Sustain The Revelation Planted Within You.* "But continue thou in the things which thou hast learned and hast been assured of, knowing of whom thou hast learned them; And that from a child thou hast known the holy scriptures, which are able to make thee wise unto

salvation through faith which is in Christ Jesus" (2 Tim. 3:14,15).

3.   *Reading The Word Of God Will Perfect Your Life.* "All scripture is given by inspiration of God, and is profitable for doctrine, for reproof, for correction, for instruction in righteousness: That the man of God may be perfect, thoroughly furnished unto all good works" (2 Tim. 3:16,17).

Picture Paul in prison. He is destitute. He has emptied his entire life. He has studied, preached, and debated. He tells Timothy to bring his coat to him in prison. He is wet and cold. He needs an extra coat. How important are his books? He writes from the prison, "bring with thee...the books, but *especially the parchments*" (2 Tim. 4:13). Above everything else he wanted was his reading materials.

Learners Become Leaders.

Leaders Are Always Readers.

4.   *Great Men Have Often Fasted Meals To Have Finances To Purchase Books.* You can spend $10 on a meal and be hungry four hours later. You can spend $10 on a book and have a *lifetime friend* that generates energy, enthusiasm, and Wisdom for the rest of your life.

Several years ago, I purchased a book for $84. One book. My young Traveling Assistant was shocked.

"I cannot believe you would pay $84 for just one book!" he exclaimed.

"Oh, son, I really did not pay $84 for a book. I purchased a man's life for $84. I will learn within two hours what took him twenty years of living and research to learn. I would be a fool not to hand the man $84 for twenty years of research."

When people seriously debate the Wisdom of

investing $20 in powerful and worthwhile books, I know their potential for success is virtually nonexistent. I have watched people pass by a life changing book saying, "I really cannot afford it." Then, watch them drive home in a $30,000 car arguing over how to pay their monthly car note.

Become informed.

Read everything you can about your Assignment.

Build the focus of your library around your Assignment. Most of your books should be linked to something God has told you to do with your life.

Recently, I walked into a home and saw a bookshelf full of books. "Oh, you love books! Have you read these books?"

"Not really," was the reply. "You see, I got them at a garage sale for $1.00." None of the books were connected to their Assignment. They simply bought books because they were inexpensive and looked good on the shelves.

Never buy a book simply because it is a bargain. Any unread book on your shelf may become emotionally burdensome. You may even feel guilty over an unread book. Refuse to collect unnecessary books.

16 Keys To Building Your Personal Wisdom Library

1. *Continuously Search For Books That Are Connected To Your Assignment.* You may find them in places you never dreamed. Used book stores often have great purchases for just a few dollars.

2. *Never Buy Retail When You Can Buy Wholesale.* Many books are being discounted in

major stores if you will look for them when you go shopping.

3. *Ask Your Mentor Which Five Books He Would Recommend Most For Your Life.*

4. *Use A Pink Highlighter Pen Continuously When You Read To Mark The Pages That Matter The Most.* Mark up the book. It is your book for learning, not for display so others will be impressed.

5. *Read Credible Authors.* "And we beseech you, brethren, to know them which labour among you, and are over you in the Lord, and admonish you" (1 Thess. 5:12).

6. *Read For A Purpose.* Read for discovery. There is a place for passive and relaxed leisurely reading. But, when you are pursuing the Wisdom of God, extract from that book everything you possibly can.

7. *Set Aside A Portion Of Your Finances Specifically For Wisdom In Your Monthly Budget.* You have budgeted for electricity, food, clothes, insurance, housing, and transportation. You will not be able to pay for any of it without Wisdom! Place Wisdom second on your budget list after the tithe.

8. *Take A Speed-Reading Course.* Invest the days and dollars to increase your speed reading skills. It has been a proven fact that those who read slowly experience wandering thoughts. The faster you read, the more you actually remember.

9. *Never Purchase A Book Without Review-ing It Thoroughly First.* I have spent money that I regretted because a book cover looked appealing. It promised more than it could deliver. Never purchase a book you have not reviewed.

10. *Never Loan Your Books To Others.* If

someone wants to Xerox a page from a reference manual, fine. They can do it on the spot. Do not let them take a book out of your home. Some of the most wonderful books I have ever owned were loaned to and lost by careless and lazy people who were too stingy to purchase their own.

11. *Establish A Separate Place Or Room As Your Personal "Wisdom Room."* (If it is a mere corner of a room, at least name it your "Wisdom Corner.")

12. *Establish A Specific Time Each Day When You Will Focus On Reading.* It may be for one hour or ten minutes, but the habit will become invaluable to your life.

13. *Keep A Microcassette Handy And Use It Daily.* Since you can talk six times faster than you can write, you will be able to gather data and file it in notebooks accordingly.

14. *Give Books As Gifts At Special Events, Holidays And Especially For Christmas Gifts.* Nothing lasts longer in the heart of another than Wisdom. Clothes are a matter of personal taste and preference. Gifts that enrich others are the gifts that are remembered. They are the gifts that truly make a lasting difference.

15. *Secure Membership Cards At Your Local Bookstore That Provide A Generous Discount.* Many bookstores today provide discounts if you are a consistent customer of that store. It pays off in the long run.

16. *Keep Receipts On Every Book Purchase.* If the book is connected to your career and calling, it could be a tax deduction.

Remember: *Your Investment In Wisdom Reveals Your Passion For Your Assignment.*

Satan's Favorite Entry Into Your Life Is Usually Through Those Closest To You.

-MIKE MURDOCK

≈ 23 ≈

YOUR RELATIONSHIPS CONTROL THE SUCCESS OF YOUR ASSIGNMENT.

You Cannot Succeed Alone.

That's why every relationship in your life should be defined and clearly understood.

18 Facts You Should Consider In Evaluating Your Relationships

1. *Your Friends Affect Your Future.* Each relationship In your life grows weeds or flowers.

2. *Each Relationship Feeds A Weakness Or A Strength.*

3. *Each Friendship Is Comfortable With Your Present Or Compatible With Your Future.*

4. *Every Relationship Is A Current That Sweeps You Toward Your Assignment Or Moves You Away From It.*

5. *Some Relationships Can Damage You Irreparably.* "And have no fellowship with the unfruitful works of darkness, but rather reprove them" (Eph. 5:11).

6. *Some Relationships Multiply Your Wisdom.* "He that walketh with wise men shall be wise: but a companion of fools shall be destroyed" (Prov. 13:20).

7. *The Purpose Of Wisdom Is To Disconnect You From Wrong People.* "For the Lord giveth Wisdom...To deliver thee from the way of the evil man...To deliver thee from the strange woman," (Prov. 2:6,12,16).

8. *Your Future Is Determined By The People You Permit Near You.*

9. *When Satan Wants To Destroy You, He Puts A Person In Your Life.*

10. *When God Wants To Promote You, He Puts A Person In Your Life.*

11. *Those Who Are Fighting Against God Will Fight Against The God In You.*

12. *Those Who Despise Obedience To God, Will Despise Your Obedience To God.*

13. *Those Who Desire God Will Recognize The God In You.*

14. *Those Who Do Not Increase You Will Inevitably Decrease You.*

15. *Those Who Do Not Make Deposits Eventually Make Withdrawals From You.* How do you discern a worthy relationship? By the Godly influence upon your Assignment.

16. *Each Friendship Will Abort Or Advance Your Assignment.*

17. *The Holy Spirit Alone Can Direct You To The Right People Who Will Assist You In Completing Your Assignment* (read Acts 8).

18. *No Relationship Is Ever Insignificant.*

You Will Need 4 Kinds Of Relationships To Succeed In Your Assignment

1. *Mentors*
2. *Protégés*

3. *Friends*
4. *Golden Connections*

8 Facts You Should Know About Mentors

1. *Mentors Are Those Who Know What You Do Not Know And Who Have Gone Where You Want To Go.* Elijah was a Mentor to Elisha. Moses was a Mentor to Joshua. Naomi was a Mentor to Ruth. Mordecai was a Mentor to Esther. Paul was a Mentor to Timothy.

2. *Your Mentor Is Your Coach, Not Your Cheerleader.* Your Mentor does not always focus on your good qualities. He is there for correction and direction. God will use others to be cheerleaders.

3. *Your Mentor Does Not Need What You Know; You Need What Your Mentor Knows.*

4. *You Are Not Essential For The Success Of Your Mentor; But He Is Essential For Your Success.*

5. *Your Mentor Is A Serious Teacher That God Uses To Correct The Course Of Your Life.*

6. *God Will Use Various Mentors At Various Times And Seasons Of Your Life.*

7. *Mentorship Is A Relationship With Someone Who Treasures Your Success Above Your Approval Of Them.*

8. *Your Mentor Will Risk Alienation In Order To Produce Your Success.*

7 Facts You Should Know About Protégés

1. *Protégés Are Those Who Will Experience Their Greatest Discoveries While With You.*

2. *Your Children Should Become Your*

Protégés.

3. *There Are Various Types Of Protégés, Just Like There Are Different Types Of Mentors.*

4. *There Are Productive Protégés And There Are Parasite Protégés.*

5. *The Uncommon Protégé Is The Student Who Receives You Continuously, Persistently, And Thankfully.*

6. *The Uncommon Protégé Listens, Obeys, And Completes Your Instructions.* Ruth obeyed Naomi and reached for Boaz. Esther obeyed Mordecai and approached the king. Elisha respected Elijah and followed him for the double portion.

7. *A Parasite Protégé Reaches For You Only During Crisis, Loss, Or Lack.* They will not necessarily follow your instructions consistently. They simply want promotion, not correction. They only associate to gain credibility through the influence of the Mentor.

7 Facts You Should Know About Friends

1. *A Friend Is The Greatest Gift God Can Give You Other Than Himself.*

2. *Your Friend Will Stay Loyal During Crisis.*

3. *Your Friend Will Be Consistent During Upheavals.*

4. *Your Friend Will Be Truthful When It Hurts.*

5. *Your Friend Is Always Accessible During Your Times Of Loneliness.*

"A friend loveth at all times, and a brother is born for adversity" (Prov. 17:17).

"Be not deceived: evil communications corrupt good manners" (1 Cor. 15:33).

6.   *Friendship Begins As A Seed.* It requires constant watering, nurturing, and protection.

7.   *A True Friend Will Increase Your Strength During Adversity.* "Two are better than one...and a threefold cord is not quickly broken" (Ecc. 4:9,12).

4 Facts To Remember About Golden Connections

1.   *Golden Connections Are Divine Bridges That Enable You To Exit From One Season And Enter Into Your Next Season Of Blessing.* The butler was a connection for Joseph to personally meet Pharaoh and interpret his dream. (See Chapter 17 for 14 Wisdom Keys you should know about the Golden Connection in your life.)

2.   *The Briefest Encounter In Your Life Can Be A Golden Link To The Greatest Dreams You Have Carried In Your Lifetime.*

3.   *Never Treat An Encounter Lightly Since God May Use It As A Golden Connection.*

4.   *God Will Move You From The Pit Into The Palace Throughout The Days Of Your Assignment... Through Golden Connections.*

Joseph discovered it. The distance from the Pit to the Palace may only be *one* person away.

Always remember, no relationship is insignificant in your life.

Remember: *Your Relationships Will Determine The Success Of Your Assignment.*

The Worth
Of Any Relationship
Can Be Measured
By Its Contributions
To Your Priorities.

-MIKE MURDOCK

∻ 24 ∻

IT IS YOUR PERSONAL RESPONSIBILITY TO INSPIRE OTHERS TO ASSIST YOU IN YOUR ASSIGNMENT.

You Will Always Need Others.
God arranged it so. You will need information, motivation, and correction throughout every season.

10 Facts You Should Know About The Law Of Asking

1.   *You Must Ask For Help.* "And I say unto you, Ask, and it shall be given you; seek, and ye shall find; knock, and it shall be opened unto you. For every one that asketh receiveth; and he that seeketh findeth; and to him that knocketh it shall be opened" (Luke 11:9,10).

2.   *You Must Ask Mentors For Counsel.* They see what you do not see. They hear what you do not hear. They have been where you have not been.

Mentors *will not* respond to your *need.*

Mentors *will* respond to your *pursuit.*

Let me explain. The Holy Spirit observes you making mistakes every day. But, He does not always correct you unless you approach Him. You must reach. You must ask, seek, and knock.

You must overcome your pride and reach for assistance. I watched a young Protégé make a mistake a few weeks ago. I had a desire to mention it to him. But, he did not want conversation, analysis, or correction. I knew it. As I attempted to discuss it, he did not have time to hear my observations. So, I waited until he tasted the pain of his error. Then, he *reached*. I responded by reviewing his mistake and offering a solution.

3. *Sinners Cannot Even Be Changed Unless They Ask Jesus To Help Them.* "Come unto Me, all ye that labour and are heavy laden, and I will give you rest. Take My yoke upon you, and learn of Me; for I am meek and lowly in heart: and ye shall find rest unto your souls. For My yoke is easy, and My burden is light" (Matt. 11:28-30).

4. *Jesus Required That The Samaritan Woman Ask.* "Jesus answered and said unto her, If thou knewest the gift of God, and Who it is that saith to thee, Give Me to drink; thou wouldest have asked of Him, and He would have given thee living water" (John 4:10). Notice this important principle. She had a need. But He could not meet that need until she pursued, reached, and *asked*. It is a Law of Life.

Pride keeps us from *reaching*.

5. *The Proof Of Humility Is The Willingness To Reach.*

I failed to grasp this Law of Asking in my early ministry. I was too proud to call a pastor and say, "I am a young evangelist. I really believe I have a message that would bless your people and inspire your church. Would you give me the privilege of coming and sharing one night with your people?" I missed a thousand opportunities because of it.

Pride is a *thief* of blessings and relationships. I was too fearful to ask partners to support my ministry with monthly Seed. I wanted approval like many young evangelists. A major pastor of a large congregation once warned me, "I hope you never ask for financial help in your newsletter." I became fearful. I knew that doors would close if ministers were unhappy with my asking friends to sow into my ministry.

I was too inexperienced to grasp that he was asking for financial support from his people three times a week! Yet, it was "wrong" for me to ask for help in my newsletter to my partners once each month!

Several years of powerful ministry were lost. I could have been on radio and television, but I was afraid to ask for financial help.

It was a wonderful and glorious day of my life when three men sat in my living room in Houston, Texas, and interrogated me. "Are you doing everything you want to do for God at this point in your ministry?"

"No, of course not," I replied.

"Well, why is your ministry not on television and radio every week reaching the thousands with the gospel?" they asked rather aggressively.

"I do not have any money to pay for the television time," was my frustrated reply.

"Then, you must have *partners*, people whom the Lord calls alongside you to hold up your hands in battle like Aaron and Hur held the hands of Moses."

Something turned on within me. I knew they were speaking truth to my heart. I just dreaded the potential alienation from certain ministers who would criticize me.

6. *You Have No Right To Anything You Have Not Pursued.* You can complain. You can gripe. You can become angry. But You Will Never Possess What You Are Unwilling To Pursue.

7. *You Must Learn To Ask Of God.* Ask Him for the tools and the resources you need to complete your Assignment.

8. *Ask God For Wisdom To Carry Out His Instructions Faithfully.* "If any of you lack Wisdom, let him ask of God, that giveth to all men liberally, and upbraideth not; and it shall be given him" (James 1:5).

9. *Ask With Great Expectation For Answers To Prayer.* "But let him ask in faith, nothing wavering. For he that wavereth is like a wave of the sea driven with the wind and tossed. For let not that man think that he shall receive any thing of the Lord. A double minded man is unstable in all his ways" (James 1:6-8).

10. *Ask God To Direct People To Participate In Your Assignment.* "Pray ye therefore the Lord of the harvest, that He will send forth labourers into His harvest" (Matt. 9:38).

▶ Champions reach. Losers withdraw.
▶ Champions network. Losers disconnect.
▶ Reaching is *not* a sign of weakness.
    Reaching is a sign of *awareness.*

The Hebrew writer penned powerful instructions, "But to do good and to communicate forget not" (Heb. 13:16).

6 Keys To Developing Communication Skills

1.   *Develop Your Speaking Skills.* Attend any class that helps you to become articulate.

2.   *Make Every Conversation Count.*

3.   *Avoid Sloppiness In Pronunciation And Expression.*

4.   *Review Your Dictionary Continually.*

5.   *Learn New Words Regularly.*

6.   *Sculpture Every Sentence In Every Conversation.*

Remember: *It Is Your Personal Responsibility To Inspire Others To Assist You In Your Assignment.*

Champions...
Simply Try Again.

-MIKE MURDOCK

❧ 25 ❧

THE SUCCESS OF YOUR ASSIGNMENT MAY REQUIRE AN ABILITY TO NEGOTIATE EFFECTIVELY WITH OTHERS.

Negotiation Begins At Birth.

When babies cry, they are negotiating for attention. Teenagers constantly negotiate with parents. Husbands and wives negotiate continuously. One dictionary says that negotiation is "to discuss with a view to reaching an agreement."

Everyone will require a measure of negotiation in their pursuit of something that really matters to them. Obviously, the levels of desire vary. The integrity of others will vary.

Some will *lie* to achieve their goal.

Some will *steal* to achieve their goal.

Some will *kill* to achieve their goal.

Some will *terminate* your friendship to achieve something else they desire.

Some will *risk their own health* to achieve something they want.

Some will risk their entire *fortune* to achieve

something they desire.

Some parents will forfeit the love of their children to achieve a goal.

Some children will walk away from their parents forever to achieve a temporary goal.

You will be continuously drawn to the negotiating table throughout your lifetime. It is like a magnet.

You cannot control the *desires* of others.

You cannot control the *behavior* of others.

You cannot *predict the price* another will pay at the negotiating table.

Negotiation is the ability to change the opinions of others through a climate of favor, instead of force. The decisions of others affect your circumstances. The city council determines the zoning of your land, whether it is residential or commercial. The salesman decides whether you purchase the car at his price or your price.

Your Assignment will always involve negotiating with others. They will have different viewpoints, experiences, and needs. Their needs will generally matter far more to them than your needs.

You cannot avoid the negotiating table. Almost every decision you make will involve others at some level. It will affect those you love financially, emotionally, physically, or even spiritually.

Uncommon negotiation occurs when you get what you desire by helping someone else get what they desire.

The Apostle Paul was a master negotiator. Educated in law, skilled in debate, and known for persuasion and logic, his writings are marvelous studies.

Pilate did not intimidate him.

Prestige did not intrigue him.

Wealth did not beckon to him.

Yet, when he spoke, kings listened and trembled.

Leadership sought him out.

His adversaries listened raptly and with great attentiveness to his viewpoints.

He knew when to be gentle, and when to be firm.

He knew when to listen, and when to speak.

He knew what to pursue, and what to avoid.

He knew a Master Key, Negotiation. His success was greatly affected by these negotiating skills.

Negotiation gifts can be developed with your family. It starts in your childhood.

Your family is the *testing ground* for your future. It may be good or it may be bad. But, your family is a gift from God to help you become qualified for enemy territory.

If you do not learn to negotiate effectively with your family, you will not negotiate effectively with your enemies.

If you learn the secrets of effective negotiation with those you love, it will inevitably affect your negotiation experiences with others in your future.

That is why the Bible has been given to us. It gives us the secrets, principles, and laws of negotiating with others.

It reveals how children are to conduct themselves toward their parents.

It is also true that many parents mistreat their children (Eph. 6:4).

The most important truth you will ever learn

in negotiating with others is to *listen for the inner voice of the Holy Spirit.* Whether you are in the presence of a serious enemy or your best friend, listen to the voice of the Holy Spirit regarding them. Jesus instructed His disciples to depend on the Holy Spirit in these times: "And when they bring you unto the synagogues, and unto magistrates, and powers, take ye no thought how or what thing ye shall answer, or what ye shall say: For the Holy Ghost shall teach you in the same hour what ye ought to say" (Luke 12:11,12).

4 Powerful Principles In The Negotiating World Of The Christian

1.   *God Anticipated Difficult Situations Where Negotiation Would Be Necessary.*
2.   *God Wants You To Be Relaxed And Unworried, But Aware That The Holy Spirit Is Present In These Scenarios Of Negotiation.*
3.   *God Desires That You Become A Learner, One Who Is Willing To Be Taught And Mentored By The Holy Spirit In Such Situations.*
4.   *God Wants You To Trust Him For The Outcome.*

20 Powerful Keys To Effective Negotiation

1.   *Never Fear What Others Can Do To You.* "For God hath not given us the spirit of fear; but of power, and of love, and of a sound mind" (2 Tim. 1:7). "In God have I put my trust: I will not be afraid what man can do unto me" (Ps. 56:11).
2.   *Concentrate On How Much Good You Can*

Do For The Other Person With Whom You Are Negotiating. "Withhold not good from them to whom it is due, when it is in the power of thine hand to do it" (Prov. 3:27).

3. *Expect God To Reward You For The Good You Do, Not The Person With Whom You Are Negotiating.* "Knowing that whatsoever good thing any man doeth, the same shall he receive of the Lord, whether he be bond or free" (Eph. 6:8).

4. *Speak Nothing That Does Not Edify And Strengthen Those At The Negotiating Table.* "Let no corrupt communication proceed out of your mouth, but that which is good to the use of edifying, that it may minister grace unto the hearers" (Eph. 4:29).

5. *Stifle Any Anger That Threatens To Enter The Negotiations.* "Let all bitterness, and wrath, and anger, and clamour, and evil speaking, be put away from you, with all malice: And be ye kind one to another, tenderhearted, forgiving one another, even as God for Christ's sake hath forgiven you" (Eph. 4:31,32).

6. *Avoid Any Attempt By Others To Make The Atmosphere Become Foolish, Lighthearted, Or Jesting.* "Neither filthiness, nor foolish talking, nor jesting, which are not convenient: but rather giving of thanks" (Eph. 5:4).

7. *Stay Alert To Any Attempt To Deceive You At The Negotiating Table.* "Let no man deceive you with vain words" (Eph. 5:6).

8. *Do Not Enter Into Any Bond, Covenant, Or Contract With The Enemies Of God.* "And have no fellowship with the unfruitful works of darkness, but rather reprove them" (Eph. 5:11).

9. *Permit The Tool Of Time To Sculpture An*

Acceptable Agreement With Others. "The Lord is good unto them that wait for Him, to the soul that seeketh Him" (Lam. 3:25).

10. *Expect The Ability And Wisdom Of God To Compensate For Your Personal Weaknesses, Limitations, And Fears.* "And I was with you in weakness, and in fear, and in much trembling. And my speech and my preaching was not with enticing words of man's Wisdom, but in demonstration of the Spirit and of power: That your faith should not stand in the Wisdom of men, but in the power of God" (1 Cor. 2:3-5).

11. *Develop The Ability To Listen Carefully To Every Word Spoken.* "A wise man will hear, and will increase learning" (Prov. 1:5). Listen to what is *not* spoken as well as words spoken. Listen for *attitudes*. Listen for areas of *pain* in others.

12. *Do Not Make Any Decision Without Sufficient Information.* "He that answereth a matter before he heareth it, it is folly and shame unto him" (Prov. 18:13).

13. *Remember The Power Of Silence.* "Even a fool, when he holdeth his peace, is counted wise: and he that shutteth his lips is esteemed a man of understanding" (Prov. 17:28).

14. *Refuse To Accept Any Gift That Could Possibly Influence The Negotiations Unwisely.* "A wicked man taketh a gift out of the bosom to pervert the ways of judgment" (Prov. 17:23).

15. *Stay Cheerful Through The Negotiation.* "A merry heart doeth good like a medicine: but a broken spirit drieth the bones" (Prov. 17:22). God will not let you fail.

16. *Do Not Share Everything You Know At The*

Negotiation Table. "He that hath knowledge spareth his words" (Prov. 17:27).

17. *Keep A Congenial But Focused Attitude Throughout The Negotiations.* "A man that hath friends must show himself friendly" (Prov. 18:24).

18. *Define Clearly Everything You Expect During The Negotiations.* "Ask, and it shall be given you: seek, and ye shall find; knock, and it shall be opened unto you" (Matt. 7:7). You have nothing to lose by asking. The worst thing that could happen when you ask someone for something is that they could reject you. If you fail to pursue something you really desire, you will live the remainder of your life wondering "what could have been."

19. *Listen Carefully To Hear What Is Loudest In The Mind Of Another.* When Abigail sent her employees to ward off David's assault on Nabal, her husband, she brought him food. Why? It was the focus of David. You must hear what another person is hearing *inside their mind*. You must listen carefully to what is *loudest* inside of them (read 1 Sam. 25).

20. *Make Certain You Understand Completely What Their Expectations Are From The Negotiations.* They have needs. Some may be overwhelming to them. Do you know what these needs are? Do you know what they cannot give up?

You, too, must not forget this powerful principle: *The Success Of Your Assignment May Require An Ability To Negotiate Effectively With Others.*

You Are
Never As Far
From A Miracle
As It First Appears.

-MIKE MURDOCK

∽ 26 ∽

YOUR ASSIGNMENT MAY OFTEN REQUIRE UNCOMMON FAVOR WITH SOMEONE.

One Day Of Favor Is Worth A Lifetime Of Labor.
Examine the life of Joseph. Year after year, he struggled for recognition from his brothers and father concerning his dream. The result? He was sold into Egypt as a slave to a passing caravan of Ishmaelites. He worked his way up in the house of Potiphar, a government official.

That is favor.

Suddenly, he experienced a horrible and terrifying chapter of false accusation. The wife of Potiphar attempted to seduce him. But he stayed true to God *and* Potiphar.

She accused him of attempted rape. He was thrust into the dungeon. He needed another current of favor. He became a model prisoner. Eventually they placed him in charge of the other prisoners. His trustworthiness had emerged, as always. He then interpreted a dream for the butler. Two years later Pharaoh called for him, and the currents of favor flowed again. Within 24 hours, Joseph went from the prison into the palace.

17 Facts You Should Know About Favor

1.   *Favor Will Bring You To Places Money Cannot Buy.* Joseph was a prisoner, not a millionaire. Yet, the favor of God brought him to the palace.

2.   *Favor Produces Miracles You Cannot Perform.* The woman with the issue of blood for 12 years had no money. But, the favor of God linked her with Jesus. Her healing was immediate when she touched His robe.

3.   *Favor Links You To Promotions For Which You Have Not Labored.* Joseph became Prime Minister in a day...because of the favor with Pharoah. One dream. One Day. It produced a lifetime promotion.

4.   *Favor Is Promised To The Obedient And Godly.* "For thou, Lord, wilt bless the righteous; with favour wilt thou compass him as with a shield" (Ps. 5:12).

5.   *Favor Can Increase In Waves In Your Life.* "And Jesus increased in Wisdom and   stature, and in favour with God and man" (Luke 2:52). "Thou hast granted me life and favour, and thy visitation hath preserved my spirit" (Job 10:12).

6.   *When You Increase In Wisdom, You Will Increase In Favor With God And Man.* "And Jesus increased in Wisdom and stature, and in favour with God and man" (Luke 2:52).

7.   *It Is Appropriate To Acknowledge And Pursue Favor.* Ruth did so with Boaz. "Then she said, Let me find favour in thy sight, my lord; for that thou hast comforted me, and for that thou hast spoken friendly unto thine handmaid, though I be not like unto one of thine handmaidens" (Ruth 2:13).

8.   *Favor Is The Essential Ingredient That*

Turns A Crisis Into A Miracle. "And it was so, when the king saw Esther the queen standing in the court, that she obtained favour in his sight: and the king held out to Esther the golden sceptre that was in his hand. So Esther drew near, and touched the top of the sceptre" (Esther 5:2). It was unlawful for Esther to approach the king when he had not called for her. It was a crucial and very critical time. She could have been put to death. Favor was the difference between death and life.

9. *Your Personal Integrity Influences The Flow Of Favor Toward You.* "Let not mercy and truth forsake thee: bind them about thy neck; write them upon the table of thine heart: So shalt thou find favour and good understanding in the sight of God and man" (Prov. 3:3,4).

10. *Doing Your Job Well Generates Favor Toward You From A Boss.* "Good understanding giveth favor" (Prov. 13:15). Diligence positions you with great men.

11. *Favor Causes The Dormant Potential Greatness Within You To Blossom And Flourish.* Just as rain causes the crops of harvest time to flourish, favor from others unlocks greatness which is hidden in you. "In the light of the king's countenance is life; and his favour is as a cloud of the latter rain" (Prov. 16:15).

12. *Favor Will Take You Further Than Money.* "A good name is rather to be chosen than great riches, and loving favour rather than silver and gold" (Prov. 22:1).

13. *Favor Births Increase And Multiplication.* When the disciples broke bread together, when they had fellowship and walked in joy praising God, favor flowed. The Lord added to the church daily while

His favor flowed. It appears that *increase* follows favor. "Praising God, and having favour with all the people. And the Lord added to the church daily such as should be saved" (Acts 2:47).

14. *Favor Turns Enemies Into Friends.* Someone is going to be good to you today! Expect it.

15. *It Takes More Than Your Gifts, Talents And Skills To Generate The Flow Of Favor.*

16. *Favor Requires God.*

Joseph was probably not the first person to interpret a dream for Pharaoh. He had people in the palace who did it for a living. But, he was the first man ever promoted to the number two position in the kingdom. *That is favor.*

Ruth was probably not the first widow Boaz ever saw gleaning in his fields. But she was the one he married. *That is favor.*

I depend completely on the favor of God in my life on a daily basis. He is the Source of everything I possess today. I do not have a thing He did not give to me.

Do you need uncommon favor today? Are you *sowing* uncommon favor toward others today? Have you started sowing favor into your mother and father? Have you honored your pastor and those in spiritual authority with significant favor?

When you want a Harvest of Favor, you must sow the Seeds of Favor.

17. *Favor Is Different Than "Favors."* Favors, are often actions designed to influence, control, and manipulate others. This is deceptive. It is the satanic substitute for the Law of Divine Favor. You see, politicians do "favors" for businessmen. You have seen it happen many times in the business world. Someone agrees to cooperate in a business deal, if

they will *exchange* advantages. These favors are actions that create a *Network of Obligation*, just like spider webs, to keep you indebted to someone.

Is anything wrong with this? Yes.

▶ You will eventually despise those who obligate you.

▶ You will always be uncomfortable in the presence of someone you *owe*.

So, move away from those who say after a meal, "I will owe you one." Or, "Do not forget now, you owe me a favor." Run for your life from those who tabulate the favors they do for you.

I am talking about something *much different*.

Favor is the attitude of *giving* to another.

Favors are the acts of *exchanging* for an anticipated advantage returned.

When you sow favor, do not obligate others to produce something in return for you. That is a business transaction. That is *not* Favor. That is an exchange.

Favor is when you sow into the life of another, knowing that the Lord of the harvest will repay you, not necessarily the person receiving from you.

▶ God is your Source.

▶ God determines the schedule He has that your harvest will arrive.

▶ God is more capable of rewarding you than anyone.

9 Important Keys In Developing The Miracle Of Favor In Your Daily Life

1. *You Must First Solve A Problem For Someone.* Favor occurs when you lift the burden off another. Joseph was trustworthy. He removed the

stress of daily business from the mind of Potiphar. Favor flowed.

When Paul prayed, he saw the healing of the father of Publius on the island of Melita. Later, he wrote that the people, "also honoured us with many honours; and when we departed, they laded us with such things as were necessary" (Acts 28:10).

When Joseph interpreted the perplexing dream of Pharaoh, promotion followed (see Gen. 41:37-45). The first thirty years of the life of Joseph were tumultuous, stormy, and violent. At the age of thirty, he became second in command of all of Egypt. Favor can bring you from sorrow to ecstasy within 24 hours.

2. *You Must Sow Favor To Create Favor.* Joseph sowed favor toward Potiphar by protecting his marriage from infidelity. God honored this.

Mordecai revealed an assassination plot against the king, and favor flowed. He sowed favor by protecting the life of the king.

Ruth labored daily to provide for her mother-in-law, Naomi. God sent Boaz to her to provide for her. Oh, believe me today! The greatest Wisdom Key that has affected my daily provision and blessing of life has been this: "What You Make Happen For Others, God Will Make Happen For You."

3. *Start Showing Favor To Everyone Close To You.* "Withhold not good from them to whom it is due, when it is in the power of thine hand to do it" (Prov. 3:27).

4. *Sow Words Of Love And Kindness Continuously To Those Around You.* "Death and life are in the power of the tongue: and they that love it shall eat the fruit thereof" (Prov. 18:21).

5. *Stay In The Center Of Your Expertise, And*

Use Your Greatest Gifts. "A man's gift maketh room for him, and bringeth him before great men" (Prov. 18:16).

6.   *When Possible, Sow Gifts Of Love Into The Lives Of Others.* "Every man is a friend to him that giveth gifts" (Prov. 19:6).

7.   *Move Swiftly To Complete An Instruction From Your Boss.* "Seest thou a man diligent in his business? he shall stand before kings; he shall not stand before mean men" (Prov. 22:29).

8.   *Respect The Rules Of Protocol, The Expected And Desired Standards Of Conduct.* Egyptians hated beards. So, "Then Pharaoh sent and called Joseph, and they brought him hastily out of the dungeon: and he shaved himself, and changed his raiment, and came in unto Pharaoh" (Gen. 41:14).

It is interesting that even table etiquette is referred to in Scripture. "When thou sittest to eat with a ruler, consider diligently what is before thee: And put a knife to thy throat, if thou be a man given to appetite" (Prov. 23:1,2).

9.   *Expect Favor Every Day Of Your Life.* "But without faith it is impossible to please Him: for he that cometh to God must believe that He is, and that He is a rewarder of them that diligently seek Him" (Heb. 11:6).

Expectation is confidence. Confidence is a current that is sensed, felt, and known. You can walk into a room and feel anger, love, or confusion. So, when you *expect* the currents of favor to flow toward you, for some unexplainable and wonderful reason, *it happens.*

Wake up each day expecting new friends to be

brought into your life.

Study the Law of Divine Favor throughout the Word of God.

Remember: *Your Assignment Will Often Require Uncommon Favor With Someone.*

❦ 27 ❦

GOD WILL NEVER PROMOTE YOU UNTIL YOU BECOME OVERQUALIFIED FOR YOUR PRESENT ASSIGNMENT.

———◆———

Your Assignment Can Change.

However, you must *become* qualified for your next season. Ruth wanted to live with Naomi. She had to qualify. Her tenacity and ability to give total focus to Naomi qualified her to move from Moab to Bethlehem.

One day, she wanted to marry Boaz. What qualified her to marry one of the wealthiest men in the city? She had carefully built a reputation of integrity and compassion. Everyone knew of her attitude toward Naomi.

She *became* qualified for Boaz.

The Secret Passage of Promotion for Daniel was the lion's den. It was the exit from Daniel's present, the gateway to his next season.

The Secret Passage of Promotion for the three Hebrew children was the fiery furnace. The three Hebrew children embraced the fiery furnace as an exit from their present and a gate into the next season.

The Secret Passage of Promotion for Joseph was false accusation. Joseph excelled in the prison after it. It was really his gate to significance.

5 Qualities That Affect Your Promotion

1.   *Excellence.* "Whatsoever thy hand findeth to do, do it with thy might" (Ecc. 9:10).

2.   *Problem Solving.* You must solve the problems that matter the most to your boss. "Withhold not good from them to whom it is due, when it is in the power of thine hand to do it" (Prov. 3:27).

3.   *Diligence.* Diligence is speedy attention to an assigned task. "He becometh poor that dealeth with a slack hand: but the hand of the diligent maketh rich" (Prov. 10:4).

"The soul of the sluggard desireth, and hath nothing: but the soul of the diligent shall be made fat" (Prov. 13:4).

4.   *Favor.* Especially with those in authority. Favor occurs when an instruction has been followed accurately and quickly. "Seest thou a man diligent in his business? he shall stand before kings; he shall not stand before mean men" (Prov. 22:29).

5.   *Cooperation.* Cooperation is getting along with others. The cause of strife is always known by others in an office. "Follow peace with all men, and holiness, without which no man shall see the Lord" (Heb. 12:14). "But foolish and unlearned questions avoid, knowing that they do gender strifes. And the servant of the Lord must not strive; but be gentle unto all men, apt to teach, patient" (2 Tim. 2:23,24).

One of the wealthiest men in America wrote an interesting article. When he sees a resumé of anyone who has difficulty in getting along with those around him, he refuses to hire the person. Their knowledge does not help. Their genius does not solve their lack of cooperation.

▶ *Survival* involves solving *your own* problems.

▶ *Promotion* involves solving the problems of *others*.

Promotion depends on the problems you are willing to solve for those around you. After Jesus addressed Peter regarding satan's desire to sift him as wheat, He gave him an instruction. It is fascinating. "But I have prayed for thee, that thy faith fail not: and when thou art converted, *strengthen thy brethren*" (Luke 22:32). Oh, my precious friend, please see this powerful principle!

An interesting experience occurred several years ago. I walked into my office after a 2,000 mile flight. I was weary and tired. A young lady who worked for me said, "May I talk to you?"

"How can I help you?"

"I need a raise," she declared emphatically.

"What do you want your raise to be?"

"I want you to pay me $1,000 a month more than what you have been paying me."

"Why?" was my puzzled and surprised reply.

"My husband and I are buying a new house and I need the money to make the payments," was her explanation.

I carefully explained to her that her salary was based on the *kind of problems* she solved. I asked her to bring me a list of the problems that she was currently solving linked to her present salary.

"When you want increased rewards, you must define your increased responsibilities," I explained.

"You are paid relative to the problems you solve for someone. The janitor may receive $12 an hour while the attorney receives $150 each hour. Their salary is not based on their personal worth, but rather on the worth of the *problem they have selected to solve* with their time, energy, and knowledge. If you want me to increase your salary, you must bring me a list of new problems you will begin to solve for me."

Obviously, this had never crossed her mind. In fact, she was not completing her *present* tasks in a timely fashion each week. She required continuous motivation from me. I had become her memo pad. She continuously forgot instructions. She required constant reminding. Her departure was not a painful experience for me whatsoever.

Even God will not promote the unqualified.

Do you want your boss to promote you?

Your *responsibilities* will increase.

Your *mistakes* become more costly.

Your *work* will be analyzed and scrutinized. "For unto whomsoever much is given, of him shall be much required: and to whom men have committed much, of him they will ask the more" (Luke 12:48).

Many employees desire equal pay with their boss. Yet, they rush out of the office the moment the clock turns 5:01 every afternoon. Their boss puts in 18 hour days. Their boss studies, reads, and carefully builds his future.

You must *qualify* for the future you are desiring.

Remember: *God Will Never Promote You Until You Become Overqualified For Your Present Assignment.*

～ 28 ～

YOUR ASSIGNMENT MAY EXPOSE YOUR PERSONAL LIMITATIONS TO REVEAL THE POWER OF GOD.

━━━►＞･◎･＜━━━

Your Assignment Is Bigger Than You Are.

When you have reached the end of yourself and exhausted your abilities, it is only *there* that the power of God becomes evident to you. This explains why He gives instructions that often leave you feeling helpless, vulnerable and even unprepared for an enemy or adversary.

Gideon felt his limitations. God reduced Gideon's army to 300 men just to reveal His divine ability and power. "So Gideon, and the hundred men that were with him, came unto the outside of the camp in the beginning of the middle watch; and they had but newly set the watch: and they blew the trumpets, and brake the pitchers that were in their hands. And the three companies blew the trumpets, and brake the pitchers, and held the lamps in their left hands, and the trumpets in their right hands to blow withal: and they cried, The sword of the Lord, and of Gideon. And they stood every man in his place round about the camp: and all the host ran, and cried, and fled. And the three hundred blew the trumpets...and the host fled...." (Judges 7:19-23).

Moses felt his personal limitations. Moses felt incompetent, inarticulate, and unintelligent when faced with his Assignment. "And Moses said unto the Lord, O my Lord, I am not eloquent, neither heretofore, nor since Thou hast spoken unto Thy servant: but I am slow of speech, and of a slow tongue" (Exodus 4:10).

It is only when you recognize your limitations, weaknesses, and vulnerabilities, that God can show His arm strong toward you.

God requires *dependency*.

The wise respond, and become *addicted* to His presence.

David felt his personal limitations. David developed a total dependency on God. He had not proven the armor of Saul. "And David girded his sword upon his armour, and he assayed to go; for he had not proved it. And David said unto Saul, I cannot go with these; for I have not proved them. And David put them off him" (1 Sam. 17:39).

But, David knew God could use a slingshot.

He moved toward his Assignment with full *dependency* upon the Lord.

David declared it to Goliath. "Then said David to the Philistine, Thou comest to me with a sword, and with a spear, and with a shield: but I come to thee in the name of the Lord of hosts, the God of the armies of Israel, whom thou hast defied. This day will the Lord deliver thee into mine hand; and I will smite thee, and take thine head from thee...that all the earth may know that there is a God in Israel...for the battle is the Lord's, and He will give you into our hands" (1 Sam. 17:45-47).

Oh, please grasp this principle! God is

determined to reveal His power to His children. When He gives you an Assignment, it will take you to the edge of your strength *where your weaknesses are fully exposed.*

It will exhaust the best in you.

It will *require* God.

Never shrink your dreams to fit your present capabilities. God does not want you to live within the realm of your own competence. His joy is to watch you move in the supernatural, fully dependent upon His love and His power in every crisis toward the completion of your Assignment.

Plan on miracles.

Your Assignment will require them.

God is not dependent upon your *gifts.*

God is not dependent upon your *knowledge.*

God is not dependent upon your *experience.*

God is not dependent upon your *friendships.*

God merely wants you fully dependent upon Him. "Not that we are sufficient of ourselves to think any thing as of ourselves; but our sufficiency *is* of God" (2 Cor. 3:5).

Remember: *Your Assignment May Expose Your Personal Limitations To Reveal The Power Of God.*

Those Who
Transfer Knowledge
Are Also Capable
Of Transferring Error.

-MIKE MURDOCK

～ 29 ～

WRONG MENTORSHIP CAN PARALYZE YOUR PROGRESS TOWARD YOUR ASSIGNMENT.

Error Is Devastating.

One small Seed of error can destroy the lifelong ministry of a godly man. I saw it happen more than 20 years ago in a small southern town. One of the leading ministers received favor, loyalty and respect from the entire town. I ministered for this precious man of God. He was admired and pursued.

His brother-in-law was an articulate and brilliant young man with unusual knowledge of Biblical languages. The brother-in-law was cynical, sarcastic, quarrelsome and continuously sowed discord regarding the doctrine of predestination. He believed that God pre-determined those who were saved or lost. You were either chosen or not. Your will had nothing to do with your eternal salvation. His militant stance on it wreaked havoc in the church of this pastor.

Obviously, such teaching makes evangelism and missionary work futile. It permits rebels to rage unchecked, uncorrected and unconverted.

Seeds grow.

Good Seed or bad Seed.

Right Seeds or wrong Seeds. Truth or error.

Anything that is sown into the soil of a human mind will grow. The mind does not referee what is right or wrong. It merely grows *any* Seed received into its soil.

It happened. The bad Seed came up. The soul winning pastor eventually resigned his church. He began a little prayer group. I watched as his influence in the community waned and died. It still stuns me today as I write this to you.

When Satan Wants To Destroy You, He Brings Someone Into Your Life. The Apostle Paul cautioned, "That we henceforth be no more children, tossed to and fro, and carried about with every wind of doctrine, by the sleight of men, *and* cunning craftiness, whereby they lie in wait to deceive" (Eph. 4:14).

Test all teaching by the entire Word of God. "Beware lest any man spoil you through philosophy and vain deceit, after the tradition of men, after the rudiments of the world, and not after Christ" (Col. 2:8).

The Test Of Truth Is By The Product It Produces.

Reject the doctrines of men. "(Touch not; taste not; handle not; Which all are to perish with the using;) after the commandments and doctrines of men?" (Col. 2:21,22).

Beware The Spirit Of Domination

Avoid the manipulation of controlling leaders. Important discipleship training has often been tainted and distorted by controlling leaders and teachers. Paul warned. "Let no man therefore judge you in meat, or in drink, or in respect of an holy day, or of the new moon, or of the sabbath *days*: Which are a shadow of things to come; but the body *is* of Christ" (Col. 2:16,17).

Let me explain. Some months ago, a young lady decided to attend my Sunday services. Her home church was several hundred miles away. She felt impressed of the Holy Spirit to come and receive more teaching on His companionship. It created a furor in her home church. She was called in by the leaders of her church and interrogated intensely. She was informed that she could not attend another church *unless her leaders had sat in services there first.*

They would not give her permission to attend. This may shock you, but it is happening in hundreds of churches across our nation today. *It is not the spiritual strength of these controlling leaders that grants that position, but the weaknesses of saints who ignorantly follow them.* "For there are many unruly and vain talkers and deceivers, specially they of the circumcision: Whose mouths must be stopped, who subvert whole houses, teaching things which they ought not, for filthy lucre's sake" (Titus 1:10,11).

Advisors *advise.*

Leaders *lead.*

Counselors *counsel.*

Controllers *control.*

Tyrants *terrorize.*

Be careful of those who desire to make your decisions for you. The True Mentor advises you but does not control you. The True Mentor does not keep you connected to him but teaches you how to develop an addiction to God Himself.

Beware Prejudiced Teaching Concerning The Holy Spirit

Prejudiced teaching against the Holy Spirit could prevent the completion of your Assignment. Jesus promised the disciples, "And I will pray the Father, and He shall give you another Comforter, that He may abide with you for ever; Even the Spirit of truth; whom the world cannot receive, because it seeth Him not, neither knoweth Him: but ye know Him; for He dwelleth with you, and shall be in you," (John 14:16,17).

I am so thankful for my unforgettable and irreplaceable companionship of the Holy Spirit. I experienced a marvelous baptism at a very young age. But, He touched my life in a dramatic and unexplainable way on July 13, 1994. I will never be the same again. I would give up every discovery, any Wisdom and knowledge I have known from childhood (including the alphabet and my ability to even speak) for what I have known and experienced through the Holy Spirit on that Wednesday at 7:00 a.m. in my bedroom.

I urge you to *pursue* a daily and hourly relationship with the Holy Spirit.

Sing to Him.

Love Him.

Talk to Him.

Discuss every part of your life with Him.

Listen to Him.

Honor Him.

The Holy Spirit is to us today what Jesus was to the twelve disciples. What Jesus is to an unbeliever, the Holy Spirit is to the believer.

The Holy Spirit is to your prayer life what Jesus is to your salvation. He *is* Life. "For in Him we live, and move, and have our being," (Acts 17:28).

The Holy Spirit is the Source of love, joy, peace and even your faith itself. "Thou wilt show me the path of life: in Thy presence is fulness of joy; at Thy right hand there are pleasures for evermore," (Ps. 16:11).

Jesus is your daily Intercessor in heaven. "Wherefore He is able also to save them to the uttermost that come unto God by Him, seeing He ever liveth to make intercession for them" (Heb. 7:25). "It is Christ that died, yea rather, that is risen again, who is even at the right hand of God, who also maketh intercession for us" (Rom. 8:34).

The Holy Spirit makes intercession for you on earth. "Likewise the Spirit also helpeth our infirmities: for we know not what we should pray for as we ought: but the Spirit Himself maketh intercession for us with groanings which cannot be uttered. And He that searcheth the hearts knoweth what is the mind of the Spirit, because He maketh intercession for the saints according to the will of God" (Rom. 8:26,27).

Any error regarding the Holy Spirit could sabotage the entire mentorship system of the Holy Spirit in your life. This could distort every experience and information entering your mind.

Beware Of False Teaching Concerning Sickness And Healing

Be alert to error regarding Divine healing.
Thousands have been taught that sickness comes
from God as a teacher. Of course, the Bible declares
that the Holy Spirit will teach us. "But the Comforter,
which *is* the Holy Ghost, whom the Father will send
in My name, He shall teach you all things, and bring
all things to your remembrance, whatsoever I have
said unto you" (John 14:26).

Jesus came to destroy the works of the devil.

Jesus healed the sick. "How God anointed Jesus
of Nazareth with the Holy Ghost and with power:
Who went about doing good, and healing all that were
oppressed of the devil; for God was with Him" (Acts
10:38).

Jesus *never* saw sickness as a teacher.

He treated disease as an *enemy*.

He *destroyed* it.

When I first entered the ministry as a church
evangelist, I was nineteen years old. I had a prayer
line during a service in south Louisiana. I can still
see the lady standing before me even now as I write.

"Do you believe God wants to heal you?" I
asked.

"Well, I believe He wants to *teach* me something
through this sickness," was her reply.

She kept refusing to embrace with great faith
the fact that God *wanted* her healed. Finally,
exasperated, I asked her, "Are you taking any
medicine?"

"Yes, I am taking lots of medicine," she replied.

"Naughty, naughty, naughty!" I teased. "If God

wants you to be sick, and He is teaching you through disease, then why are you sneaking behind His back trying to get well?"

If God wants you ill, every doctor, nurse, and hospital is a monument of rebellion and defiance to His plan.

Beware False Teaching Regarding Poverty And Prosperity

Much error is being taught regarding financial blessing. Some teach that if you are truly serving the Lord with all of your heart, your wealth is guaranteed. Yet, thousands of the wealthy are complete rebels to the will of God. Jesus often warned the rich and those who desired to be wealthy. "Take heed, and beware of covetousness: for a man's life consisteth not in the abundance of the things which he possesseth" (Luke 12:15).

James warned, "Your riches are corrupted, and your garments are motheaten. Your gold and silver is cankered; and the rust of them shall be a witness against you, and shall eat your flesh as it were fire. Ye have heaped treasure together for the last days" (James 5:2,3).

Wealth is not necessarily the proof of obedience nor the approval of God.

Yet, in contradiction to this, some have swung the pendulum the other way.

Some feel guilty for pursuing financial blessing and abundance. Yet, financial promises are continuously made in Scripture to those who enter into a covenant of sowing and reaping with the Lord of the harvest.

Provision is promised to the sower. "Give, and it shall be given unto you; good measure, pressed down, and shaken together, and running over, shall men give into your bosom. For with the same measure that ye mete withal it shall be measured to you again" (Luke 6:38).

Protection is promised to the tither. "Bring ye all the tithes into the storehouse, that there may be meat in Mine house, and prove Me now herewith, saith the Lord of hosts, if I will not open you the windows of heaven, and pour you out a blessing, that there shall not be room enough to receive it. And I will rebuke the devourer for your sakes, and he shall not destroy the fruits of your ground; neither shall your vine cast her fruit before the time in the field, saith the Lord of hosts" (Malachi 3:10,11).

Plenty is promised to givers. "Honour the Lord with thy substance, and with the firstfruits of all thine increase: So shall thy barns be filled with plenty, and thy presses shall burst out with new wine" (Prov. 3:9,10).

Blessing is promised to the obedient. "And it shall come to pass, if thou shalt hearken diligently unto the voice of the Lord thy God, to observe and to do all His commandments which I command thee this day, that the Lord thy God will set thee on high above all nations of the earth: And all these blessings shall come on thee, and overtake thee, if thou shalt hearken unto the voice of the Lord thy God" (Deut. 28:1,2).

"If God really wants me to have money, He will give it to me," was the sardonic observation of a cynic in a recent crusade.

"Yes, I understand your philosophy. If He

wanted your hair combed, He would have combed it for you this morning," was my reply.

Another cynic said, "Dr. Mike, don't you believe the devil will give you a lot of money to make you backslide away from God?"

"Then, why has he not overdosed you with finances?" was my reply. When satan wanted to destroy Job, he did not double his income. He stole it.

What satan steals, God returns double. Read Job 42 very carefully. Read it aloud. Read it often. "And the Lord turned the captivity of Job, when he prayed for his friends: also the Lord gave Job twice as much as he had before...So the Lord blessed the latter end of Job more than his beginning" (Job 42:10-17).

God *blessed* him.

God *provided.*

God gave him *finances.*

God gave him *provision.*

Jesus described His difference from false prophets very clearly. "The thief cometh not, but for to steal, and to kill, and to destroy: I am come that they might have life, and that they might have it more abundantly" (John 10:10).

Your Heavenly Father is well aware of your financial needs. "Your heavenly Father knoweth that ye have need of all these things" (Matt. 6:32).

Jesus taught that spiritual priorities produce provision. "But seek ye first the kingdom of God, and His righteousness; and all these things shall be added unto you" (Matt. 6:33). The teaching of Jesus was twofold: First, the Provider. Second, the Provision.

Jesus taught that our Father was a Giver, the

true Source of every good and perfect gift. "If ye then, being evil, know how to give good gifts unto your children, how much more shall your Father which is in heaven give good things to them that ask Him?" (Matt. 7:11).

Second, Jesus taught that obedience produces supernatural provision for you. "But seek ye first the kingdom of God, and His righteousness; and all these things shall be added unto you" (Matt. 6:33).

Oh, run from error! Refuse to even receive it into your spirit or mind. Never negotiate with falsehood.

One Seed In The Mind Can Destroy A Lifetime Of Blessing.

4 Keys In Discerning Error

1. *You Must Study The Word Of God For Yourself.* "Study to show thyself approved unto God, a workman that needeth not to be ashamed, rightly dividing the Word of truth" (2 Tim. 2:15). Studying truth births the recognition of error.

2. *Refuse Conversation With Those Who Are Obsessed With Questions Instead Of Solutions.* "But shun profane *and* vain babblings: for they will increase unto more ungodliness...But foolish and unlearned questions avoid, knowing that they do gender strifes. And the servant of the Lord must not strive; but be gentle unto all *men*, apt to teach, patient" (2 Tim. 2:16,23,24).

3. *Enter The Secret Place And Listen To The Holy Spirit, Your Mentor* (read John 14-16). One hour with the Holy Spirit will transform your discerning ability.

4. *Recognize That Truth Will Bring Joy And Great Liberty; Error Brings Bondage, Fear, And Depression.* "And ye shall know the truth, and the truth shall make you free" (John 8:32).

4 Facts About The Spirit Of Error

▶ Error enters your life through a *person*.
▶ Error enters your life during a season of *great need*.
▶ Error enters your life to *distract* you.
▶ Error increases agitation, frustration, and *fear*.

"For the vile person will speak villany, and his heart will work iniquity, to practice hypocrisy, and to utter error against the Lord, to make empty the soul of the hungry, and he will cause the drink of the thirsty to fail" (Isa. 32:6).

The secret of the obedient life is not in understanding error, but in pursuing *truth*.

When I was young, I encountered great internal frustration in my pursuit of truth. I always had a fear of believing a lie. I was quite concerned that perhaps I was influenced too greatly by my parents.

I reasoned, "What if Daddy is wrong? What if Mother is merely repeating the teachings she has heard from her childhood? How do I *really* know if I am following the *truth*?"

So I began to gather various books on different cults, religions, and belief systems. I wanted to study them for myself. I was defiant, rebellious, and insistent that *everybody* had a view worth considering.

While in prayer, the Holy Spirit revealed a

powerful truth to me: *It is impossible to understand error.* You have to be perverted to accept the perversion. My exhaustive study of cults, doctrines of men and belief systems would not bring me to a satisfying conclusion.

Jesus alone was Truth.

When Truth consumes you, error has no place within you. A friend told me that when bank tellers are being taught to distinguish counterfeit money, they are not given any phony money. Rather, they are given piles and piles of real money, *genuine* currency, to handle. When they have handled genuine currency repeatedly enough and something the counterfeit is recognized *instantly*. They discern the false money because they have studied the genuine currency.

The Word of God is the true standard for discerning error. Absorb His Word and His presence so often that when something *contrary* to the Holy Spirit enters, *you will discern it instantly*. "Lest satan should get an advantage of us: for we are not ignorant of his devices" (2 Cor. 2:11).

Our Prayer Together...

"Father, I pray for every special friend today who is reading Your revelation on his Assignment. I ask You to reveal truth in every part of his life. Reveal truth about Your healing presence, Your financial provision, and about the Holy Spirit. Do not let us continue in any error. We hate falsehood and every evil way. We despise the doctrines of men but hunger for righteousness. *Purify our minds,* sanctify our hearts, and provide a wall of protection around us that we would never fall into the pitfalls of prejudiced teaching, erroneous teaching, and error. We have confidence that You will *protect* our minds and hearts, and will keep us focused on total obedience to Your plan for our lives. Make the Word come alive in us. Let Your words be like fire to purge and burn out anything unlike You. Help us to conquer and destroy the carnal and fleshly nature of our lives and permit the Holy Spirit to consume us. I ask this humbly and with all that is within me, in Jesus' name. Amen."

Remember: *Wrong Mentorship Can Paralyze Your Progress Toward Your Assignment.*

Pain Is Not An Enemy
But Merely
The Proof
That One Exists.

-MIKE MURDOCK

～ 30 ～
WHEN YOU DISCOVER YOUR ASSIGNMENT, YOU WILL DISCOVER YOUR ENEMY.

You Will Always Have An Enemy.

When Joseph discovered his Assignment and shared it with his brothers, they quickly reacted. They sold him into slavery.

When Esther became queen, she soon discovered Haman. He was the enemy of her people, the Jews. He was conspiring to destroy them all.

When Nehemiah received permission from the king to rebuild the walls of Jerusalem, his enemies emerged. The warfare began.

When Jesus was born in Bethlehem, King Herod immediately took action to have Him killed.

When Jesus began His active ministry, the Pharisees opposed Him at every turn and eventually agreed with His crucifixion.

Discovering your Assignment is wonderful, energizing, and thrilling. Watching the Miracle Hand of God connect you with strategic relationships is so stimulating and exciting.

But, you have an enemy.

You will *always* have an enemy.

Your enemy has recognized your Assignment.

9 Facts You Should Know About Your Assignment And Your Enemy

The Goal Of Your Enemy Is Broken Focus.

1. *Do Not Permit Your Focus To Be Shifted To Your Enemy.*

"Mike, I was so excited about my new church," the words gushed out of a young preacher's mouth late one night as we talked in his living room. "I felt like this was heaven on earth. The people loved me. My family loved the new city. Everything was perfect. Then, suddenly out of nowhere one of the men of the church spread a false accusation against me. It has devastated me. I do not know which way to turn. What should I do? Did I *miss* the will of *God*?"

"Actually, this probably *confirms* that you are in the center of the will of God," I replied.

His enemy had *reacted.*

2. *Every Move In The Right Direction Will Be Confronted By Your Enemy.* Demons are assigned geographically just like angels and humans. When satan discovers that you are pursuing the center of your Assignment, demons will be assigned to prevent your entry into the next season, break your focus and *dilute your joy.*

3. *Recognize The Value Of An Enemy.* Your enemy is a *signpost* permitted by God to *confirm* that you are truly *entering* the greatest season of your life.

4. *Your Enemy Causes Movement.* The

Israelites would have remained in Egypt had their afflictions not become unbearable.

5. *Your Enemy Reveals The Necessity Of God.* Without a conflict, we often become arrogant, self-centered and self-sufficient.

6. *Your Enemy Is The Only Obstacle Between Obscurity And Greatness.* David, without a Goliath, was just another shepherd boy. After he killed Goliath, he was known to all Israel.

7. *Your Assignment Forces Your Enemy To Reveal Himself.* As Jesus obeyed the Father, preaching and healing the sick, His enemies could not stifle their reaction and hatred.

8. *Your Enemy Forces Your Future To Become Visible.* Goliath positioned David for visibility. His future as a military champion became established.

9. *Your Enemy Is An Announcement That The Future You Have Longed For Has Arrived.* Goliath provided David an opportunity to demonstrate his difference from others.

Remember: *When You Discover Your Assignment, You Will Discover Your Enemy.*

You Will Never Be
Promoted
Until You Have Become
Over-Qualified
For Your Present
Assignment.

-MIKE MURDOCK

⮞ 31 ⮜

YOUR RISE TO LEADERSHIP WILL REQUIRE EXCELLENCE IN YOUR PRESENT ASSIGNMENT.

Leadership Is Earned.

Before Ruth became the wife of wealthy Boaz, she *served* as a handmaiden to Naomi, her mother-in-law (read Ruth 1-4).

Before Joseph became second in command of Egypt, he *served* Potiphar and the prison system (see Gen. 39-41).

Before David became king of Israel, he *served* King Saul (see 1 Sam. 16:14-23).

Jesus taught that serving well decides your rise to greatness. "But whosoever will be great among you, let him be your minister; And whosoever will be chief among you, let him be your servant" (Matt. 20:26,27). Jesus instructed His disciples that whoever wanted to be greatest among them must *first* become their servant. Sometimes you want to prosper first, then serve. But Jesus taught that servanthood preceded promotion.

Leadership is earned through servanthood.

Arrogance can cost you your Assignment. When King Saul ceased to have the heart of a servant, he ceased to prosper.

Uncommon Leaders have simply recognized the value of others. Humility is not thinking you are worthless. It is recognition of the worth and value of *others.* It is the willingness to help someone else succeed even if it requires that you step aside.

Your willingness to suffer qualifies you for eventual rulership. "If we suffer, we shall also reign with *Him*: if we deny *Him* He also will deny us" (2 Tim. 2:12).

4 Important Facts About Excellence In Serving

"Humble yourselves therefore under the mighty hand of God, that He may exalt you in due time" (1 Peter 5:6).

▶ Servanthood is *instructed* by God.
▶ Servanthood is *expected* by God.
▶ Servanthood will always be *rewarded* at the appropriate time.
▶ Servanthood eventually becomes *rulership.*

Remember: *Your Rise To Leadership Will Require Excellence In Your Present Assignment.*

Our Prayer Together...

"Father, use these Seeds of Wisdom on Assignment to grow an uncommon harvest of peace, productivity and supernatural love for others. Use us to heal, restore, strengthen and bring many into a life of total obedience to You. We give ourselves to You and the Assignment You have commanded. In Jesus' name. Amen."

Your Letter Is Very Important to Me

You are a special person to me, and I believe that you are special to God. I want to assist you in any way possible. Write me when you need an intercessor to pray for you. When you write, my staff and I will pray over your letter. I will write you back.

Mike, please enter into the prayer of agreement with me for the following needs:
(Please Print)

_____

_____

_____

_____

_____

_____

_____

_____

_____

_____

_____

_____

_____

_____

Mail to:
The Wisdom Center • *P. O. Box 99* •*Denton, TX 76202*
Phone: 1-888-WISDOM-1 (1-888-947-3661)
Website: **www.thewisdomcenter.cc**

WISDOM 12 PAK

THE MASTER SECRET OF LIFE IS WISDOM

Ignorance Is The Only True Enemy Capable Of Destroying You (Hosea 4:6, Proverbs 11:14)

▶ 1.	MY PERSONAL DREAM BOOK	B143	$5.00
▶ 2.	THE COVENANT OF FIFTY EIGHT BLESSINGS	B47	$8.00
▶ 3.	WISDOM, GOD'S GOLDEN KEY TO SUCCESS	B71	$7.00
▶ 4.	SEEDS OF WISDOM ON THE HOLY SPIRIT	B116	$5.00
▶ 5.	SEEDS OF WISDOM ON THE SECRET PLACE	B115	$5.00
▶ 6.	SEEDS OF WISDOM ON THE WORD OF GOD	B117	$5.00
▶ 7.	SEEDS OF WISDOM ON YOUR ASSIGNMENT	B122	$5.00
▶ 8.	SEEDS OF WISDOM ON PROBLEM SOLVING	B118	$5.00
▶ 9.	101 WISDOM KEYS	B45	$7.00
▶ 10.	31 KEYS TO A NEW BEGINNING	B48	$7.00
▶ 11.	THE PROVERBS 31 WOMAN	B49	$7.00
▶ 12.	31 FACTS ABOUT WISDOM	B46	$7.00

Wisdom Is The Principal Thing

Book Pak
WBL-12 / $30
(A $73 Value!)

The Wisdom Center

Learn From The Greatest.

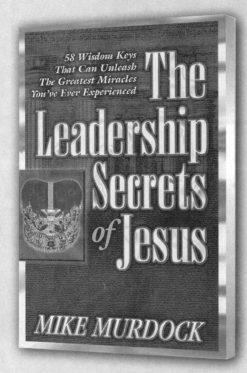

58 Wisdom Keys That Can Unleash The Greatest Miracles You've Ever Experienced

The Leadership Secrets of Jesus

MIKE MURDOCK

▶ The Secret Of Handling Rejection

▶ How To Deal With The Mistakes Of Others

▶ 5 Power Keys For Effective Delegation To Others

▶ The Key To Developing Great Faith

▶ The Greatest Qualities Of Champions

▶ The Secret Of The Wealthy

▶ Four Goal-Setting Techniques

▶ Ten Facts Jesus Taught About Money

In this dynamic and practical guidebook Mike Murdock points you directly to Jesus, the Ultimate Mentor. You'll take just a moment every day to reflect on His life and actions. And when you do, you'll discover all the key skills and traits that Jesus used... the powerful "leadership secrets" that build true, lasting achievement. Explore them. Study them. Put them to work in your own life and your success will be assured!

Wisdom Is The Principal Thing
Book B-91 / $10
The Wisdom Center

You can have it.

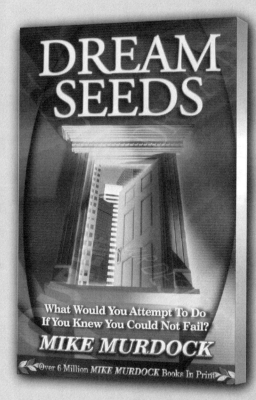

▶ **Why Sickness Is Not The Will Of God**

▶ **How To Release The Powerful Forces That Guarantee Blessing**

▶ **The Incredible Role Of Your Memory And The Imagination**

▶ **The Hidden Power Of Imagination And How To Use It Properly**

▶ **The Difference Between The Love Of God And His Blessings**

▶ **3 Steps In Increasing Your Faith**

▶ **2 Rewards That Come When You Use Your Faith In God**

▶ **7 Powerful Keys Concerning Your Faith**

Dreams and desires begin as photographs within our hearts and minds things that we want to happen in our future. God plants these pictures as invisible Seeds within us. God begins every miracle in your life with a Seed-picture… the invisible idea that gives birth to a visible blessing. In this teaching, you will discover your desires and how to concentrate on watering and nurturing the growth of your Dream-Seeds until you attain your God-given goals.

Wisdom Is The Principal Thing

Book B-11 / **$9**

Six Audio Tapes TS-2 / **$30**

The Wisdom Center

Run To Win.

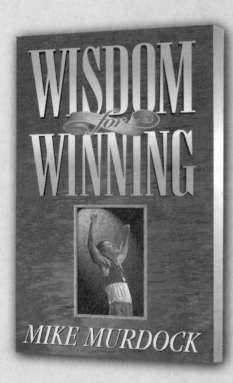

▶ 10 Ingredients For Success

▶ Ten Lies Many People Believe About Money

▶ 20 Keys For Winning At Work

▶ 20 Keys To A Better Marriage

▶ 3 Facts Every Parent Should Remember

▶ 5 Steps Out Of Depression

▶ The Greatest Wisdom Principle I Ever Learned

▶ 7 Keys To Answered Prayer

▶ God's Master Golden Key To Total Success

▶ The Key To Understanding Life

Everyone needs to feel they have achieved something with their life. When we stop producing, loneliness and laziness will choke all enthusiasm from our living. What would you like to be doing? What are you doing about it? Get started on a project in your life. Start building on your dreams. Resist those who would control and change your personal goals. Get going with this powerful teaching and reach your life goals!

Wisdom Is The Principal Thing

Book B-01 / $10

Six Audio Tapes TS-01 / $30

The Wisdom Center

THE SECRET.

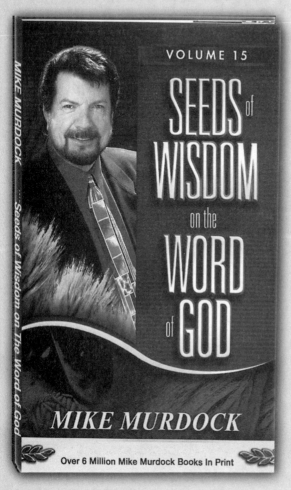

VOLUME 15

SEEDS of
WISDOM
on the
WORD
of GOD

MIKE MURDOCK

Over 6 Million Mike Murdock Books In Print

▶ 11 Reasons Why
The Bible Is The
Most Important
Book On Earth

▶ 12 Problems The
Word Of God
Can Solve In
Your Life

▶ 4 Of My Personal
Bible Reading
Secrets

▶ 4 Steps To
Building A
Spiritual Home

▶ 9 Wisdom Keys
To Being
Successful In
Developing The
Habit Of Reading
The Word Of
God

Wisdom Is The Principal Thing

Book
B-117 / $5

The Wisdom Center